THE INNER SUBURBS

THE INNER SUBURBS

The evolution of an industrial area

BERNARD BARRETT

MELBOURNE UNIVERSITY PRESS

First published 1971
Printed in Australia by
Halstead Press Pty Ltd, Kingsgrove, N.S.W. 2208 for
Melbourne University Press, Carlton, Victoria 3053
Great Britain and Europe: ISBS Inc., London
USA and Canada: ISBS Inc., Portland, Oregon 97208
Registered in Australia for transmission by post as a book
Designed by Norman Quaintance

ISBN 0 522 84013 2
Dewey Decimal Classification Number 309.1945

For my wife, Jeanne,
and my children,
Katrina and Gavin

PREFACE

This book presents a facet of Australian history which has not been exposed before, or certainly not in such disgusting detail. It tells of an incident in the early days of pollution in Australia. A few years ago such a subject may not have aroused much interest. Today, alarm over the increasing environmental decay, in all its forms, is a vital issue—one kind of social unrest that is not contentious. Politicians of the right and the left, student activists and academics, evangelists and atheists—all may agree that the accelerating destruction of the earth's resources cannot be regarded as a good thing to be encouraged by lax laws. It is valuable to be reminded that the process which is now so obvious to everyone started long before the advent of cars and other mechanisms of this century. The destructive influence of the industrial revolution, in its last late colonial fling, was well advanced one century ago. Our great-grandfathers' methods were different from ours. They were polluters of a crude and clumsy, personal kind. We are more sophisticated and impersonal and generally our efforts are less shockingly visible, while the winds keep blowing; altogether we work on a much grander scale. But this does not detract from interest in the work of amateurs.

Mr Barrett's thesis challenges the widely accepted view that the depressed areas of urban Australia have, in a sense, only themselves to blame: that Australia heaped them with all her usual blessings at the start but they somehow took a wrong turning, and gradually deteriorated. On the contrary, some of them were doomed from the beginning—were in fact set apart, by the cynical, realistic reasoning of nineteenth-century commerce, to be slums from the outset.

Collingwood, close to Melbourne's 'Golden Mile', the central example studied in this book, was one such district. It was born with a wooden spoon in its mouth, but not because it was underprivileged by nature. It occupied the morning side of a pleasant hill with a river at its foot. It just happened to be a convenient backyard where a busy adolescent town could sweep its junk more or less out of sight, if not always out of smell.

This is a fascinatingly dirty book. The poor, misused heroine is that little river at the foot of the hill: the Yarra. At the start of the story, it is a modest but pretty, pure, sparkling, tree-lined stream. The description of its desecration, in a few years, by floods of blood and offal, night-soil, and the wastes of tanneries, fellmongers, soap and candle makers, is as hair raising as melodrama. (Meanwhile, over the hill to the west, they were laying out the Botanic Gardens and planting trees outside the classical facades of Collins Street.)

A modern reader may experience a sort of twisted satisfaction from the story, by the realization that there were other times, not so long ago, when good citizens were even more insensitive to the immediate devastation they were creating than most good citizens are now. And since it is easier to recognize blindness, mean expediency, base motives—and the rare exceptions—when they are a generation removed, every detail of this sordid story makes relevant and salutary reading today.

ROBIN BOYD

ACKNOWLEDGMENTS

In the early stages of this research I was fortunate to receive advice and encouragement from Weston Bate, Dr Graeme Davison and Dr Joy Parnaby. I am grateful to the staff of the various libraries and public offices, who helped me to locate sources. My inquiries in the suburbs were greatly helped by Andrew McCutcheon, architect, who is a member of Collingwood City Council; Mr Dudley Cook, Town Clerk of Collingwood; the Reverend Bruce Anderson, formerly of Collingwood, who was a member of Collingwood City Council; and Mr Jack O'Halloran, formerly Town Clerk of Fitzroy, now of Prahran. At the stage of writing and revising, I have had the benefit of comments from Robin Boyd and Dr Geoffrey Serle. Parts of the manuscript have been read by Jim Rundle, Renate Howe, Elaine Martin, Howard Deakin, Brian Kiernan, John Lack, Don Garden, Don Gibb and George Legge. George Price prepared the maps and diagrams. Most of all, I am indebted to my wife, Jeanne, who participated in all the roles mentioned above, and to my children, Katrina and Gavin, for their patience.

CONTENTS

ILLUSTRATIONS

Australia is a significant instance of urbanization. By 1880, a hundred years after the first white settlement, Australia comprised one of the most urbanized communities in the world, with half of its population living in cities and towns. Today four-fifths of Australians live in such areas, and more than half live in the four largest cities. Asa Briggs, the English writer on comparative urban development, visited Australia in 1960 and commented:

> Australia should be a world centre of urban studies. An exceptionally high proportion of Australians are urban creatures. Each Australian city is young enough to have its life history examined in detail and old enough to have a life history which is interesting. The urban experience and problems of the different Australian cities have much in common, but there are significant and illuminating variations. Geographers, historians, sociologists and economists should co-operate with 'practical' specialists on cities—town planners, architects, social workers and journalists—to explore 'the culture of cities' in its Australian setting. The results would be of interest to students of cities and city-dwellers in all parts of the world.[1]

Among historians, there is increasing awareness of the importance of urban development in Australian history. From the work of N. G. Butlin, *Investment in Australian Economic Development, 1861–1900* (1964), it is clear that Australian economic development in the second half of the nineteenth century was based largely on the building of cities. Much private and public capital, and much labour, went into providing houses, shops, offices, churches, streets, drains, hospitals, town halls, suburban transport, piped water, gas street-lighting and sanitation. Indeed, in Australia's case, it seems, this urban development tended to stimulate industrialization rather than the reverse. Accordingly, future writings about Australian history will probably give greater attention than before to urban life. In an article reviewing the state of Australian urban studies in 1970, George Clarke (a consultant town planner) shows that there is scope for much more research into the question: pre-

B

cisely how, when and why did Australians adopt the suburban mode of living?[2]

One theme of special interest for students of comparative urban development is the shaping of the environment. Why are some neighbourhoods for the rich and others for the poor? Why are some neighbourhoods chiefly residential, i.e. areas of consumption, while others concentrate on production? What are the origins of slums and urban pollution?

Several geographical patterns have been distinguished in metropolitan areas. Sometimes the metropolis seems to consist of concentric zones, with the lower ranks of society concentrated in the inner areas and the middle and upper ranks dispersed outwards. A classic description of this pattern was made in the 1920s by Ernest Burgess, of the pioneering school of urban studies at the University of Chicago.[3] In another pattern, pointed to by later writers, a metropolis may be arranged in sectors (or 'quarters' as they are often called in older countries). Each sector extends outwards from its original centre and has a certain socio-economic and possibly ethnic character.

In Australia it is easy to find prima facie evidence of both patterns. Take, for example, recent studies of the status of suburbs in Sydney and Melbourne. Athol Congalton, of the University of New South Wales, investigated public opinion concerning 368 localities listed in a Sydney metropolitan street directory.[4] F. Lancaster Jones, of the Australian National University, analysed the 1961 census data and ranked 133 Melbourne localities according to their possession of occupational, religious and ethnic characteristics said to be associated with high or low status.[5] Looking at the resulting lists and comparing them with metropolitan maps, the reader notices an interesting geographical arrangement.

In the Sydney study, the ten lowest-ranking localities (in descending order: Zetland, Erskineville, Alexandria, Macdonaldtown, Ultimo, Waterloo, Pyrmont, Woolloomooloo, Surry Hills and Redfern) are inner industrial areas, forming an arc south of the central business district. Of the ten highest-ranking localities (in descending order: Vaucluse, Point Piper, Darling Point, Bellevue Hill, Pymble, Palm Beach, Potts Point, Killara, Wahroonga and Beauty Point), five are eastern and five are northern—all with good scenery.

In Melbourne, the lowest-ranking suburbs (according to Jones's criteria) are the old ones, forming a ring within two miles or so of the General Post Office (reading clockwise: North Melbourne,

Carlton, Fitzroy, Collingwood, Richmond, South Melbourne, Port Melbourne). To the west and north of Melbourne (from Williamstown to Preston) there are sectors of medium-status suburbs, again largely industrial. These sectors in general have a flat, dull landscape, with soil often poor, sometimes rocky. Melbourne's highest-ranking suburbs are situated in sectors extending to the east and south—in the direction of hills and beaches. These suburbs generally have better soil or better scenery.

Statistical studies such as these are interesting, but are in danger of being superficial. They need to be supplemented and corrected by detailed studies of particular places.

When Australians wonder about the origin of industrial or slum areas, they usually adopt a convenient blanket explanation. According to this, the poor areas were originally genteel or fashionable; they decayed as the gentry moved out to create new suburbs and as the poor took their place; solid mansions were subdivided into apartment houses or boarding houses; verandas were stripped of their ornamental cast-iron lace and boarded up to make sleep-outs; meanwhile, factories sprang up, attracting still more poor people to the district.[6] This theory of senility and gradual decay may fit reality in many places, but it fails to account for certain significant exceptions. It describes only one kind of urban environment. This book insists that there is another kind of urban environment—a neighbourhood spoilt from the outset, crippled from birth. Just as the theory of concentric zones needs to be supplemented by a theory of sectors, so the theory of senile suburbs needs to be supplemented by a theory of crippled suburbs.

Australia's first suburbs developed in Sydney and there we find examples of both environments—the crippled and the merely senile. This Sydney background is worth looking at as it will help us to understand the detailed study of Melbourne which is our main concern.

Shortly after the first white settlement in Sydney harbour in 1788, convicts overflowed from the central official quarters and sought shelter on a nearby peninsula, known as the Rocks, near the southern end of today's Harbour Bridge. The Rocks area was too barren for agriculture and too steep for horse-drawn transport or commerce. Water was scarce there and sanitation difficult. Houses were scattered about without much order. As free settlers increased in Sydney, the Rocks area was shunned by the higher classes and became a rendezvous for the poorest—the birthplace of Australia's

3

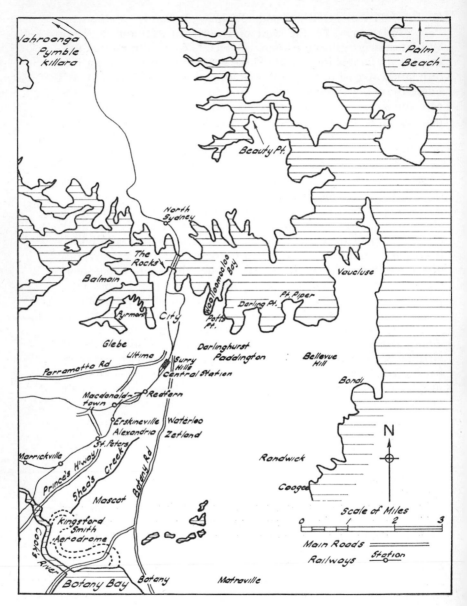

Sydney and inner suburbs.

proletariat. Thus crippled, the Rocks was Australia's first slum. Late in the nineteenth century it gained a further notoriety as a home of larrikins, the rowdy adolescents who terrorized Sydney streets. Since then the Rocks has been changing. Many houses, including the worst, were condemned and demolished after a plague scare in 1900, and whole streets were demolished about 1930 to make way for the Harbour Bridge. Today, with a shortage of building sites in Sydney's central business district, the Rocks is being considered for redevelopment because of its convenient location and its harbour views.

During the settling of the Rocks area, the upper classes of early Sydney moved out a mile or so in other directions—in a belt extending from Darlinghurst to Glebe. Here the well-drained slopes were considered healthy places to live. Compared with the Rocks, this zone is nearer to the popular notion of urban decay. Between 1860 and 1890 the elite areas fell in the social scale as speculators and builders subdivided spacious grounds and erected tightly packed houses (including double-storey terraces) for the middle classes and artisans. By the end of the century the middle classes were moving out to new subdivisions, leaving the terraces to the workers.

However, the pattern of Sydney's industrial suburbs is as much 'sectorial' as concentric. The first major industrial region developed to the south, towards Botany. This direction was attractive to industry because of the comparatively level ground, ample water supplies and ready means of waste disposal. Shea's Creek, which originally carried pure water, began a couple of miles from Sydney, near Redfern, and flowed southward into Cook's River, which in turn meandered prettily into Botany Bay. On the shores at Botany were some perpetual freshwater springs and lakes. The bay served as a ready-made cesspool.

This industrialization did not all spread from the city outwards. The Botany end was industrial from the outset. Indeed, it was the birthplace of Australia's private industry. In 1815, near the outfall of the lakes, Simeon Lord (merchant and ex-convict) built wool-washing and weaving works, with houses for himself and his workers. In 1818 a paper mill opened nearby, followed by other woolwashers, fellmongers and tanners. Because of the remoteness from Sydney, nuisances went unchecked. However, manufacturing did not develop so rapidly in New South Wales (a free-trade colony) as it did later in Victoria, where protective tariffs were established. The mill established by Lord closed in 1856, to the joy of British manufacturers and Australian importers of woollen cloth.

In the twentieth century, Sydney's industrial growth has been stimulated by the federation of Australia and the adoption of nationwide protection policies, as well as by two world wars. Much of this industrialization has been concentrated at Botany and in the comparatively level Waterloo-Alexandria-Marrickville area, between Botany and Sydney. Shea's Creek is now a drainage channel, and the mouth of Cook's River has been straightened to provide space for Sydney's airport. The Botany region has lost its botany, and is beset with pollution problems.

Melbourne's development resembles Sydney's in some ways—in the common problems of housing, industry, sanitation, pollution and the location of suburbs. But Melbourne's development has been concentrated into a shorter period. Melbourne was founded in 1835-7—fifty years after Sydney and about the same time as Adelaide. (Brisbane and Perth were settled in the 1820s, laid out in the 1840s and developed slowly after that.) As Victoria was the colony most affected by the gold rushes of the 1850s and by consequent economic activities, Melbourne soon surpassed Sydney in size. By 1861 Melbourne and suburbs had 139,916 people, compared with Sydney's 95,789. Melbourne remained Australia's biggest city (with 496,079 people in 1901) until Sydney regained the ascendancy after 1901. When Asa Briggs wrote *Victorian Cities* (1963), comparing six British cities that developed during the heyday of the Empire, he made a point of including one Victorian-era city overseas, and he chose Melbourne. 'Melbourne', he wrote, 'is one of the most interesting cities of the Empire.'

Before 1850, today's inner suburbs (those within two miles of Melbourne's General Post Office) were a rural-urban fringe, more rural than urban. These districts received an overflow of population from Melbourne during Victoria's gold immigration of 1852-4. During the next generation or so, they held the bulk of Melbourne's population. Some parts of this zone (for example, Carlton, southern Fitzroy and western Richmond) do conform to the popular notion—that is, they were originally genteel but eventually deteriorated to become working-class. But there are significant exceptions. Parkville (a small community on the western fringe of Carlton, adjoining the University of Melbourne) and East Melbourne are still attractive, and the northern half of South Yarra is still one of Melbourne's most desirable addresses.

Melbourne and suburban municipalities.

The most interesting exception of all is Collingwood, Melbourne's classic case of a suburb crippled from birth. The difference between Collingwood and its neighbours is partly one of topography. Carlton, southern Fitzroy and western Richmond are elevated and therefore always had good natural means of drainage, but, unlike the Rocks, they were not discouragingly steep. Their dryness (or 'healthiness' as it was called in the mid-nineteenth century) made them valuable real estate. Most of Collingwood, on the other hand, is surprisingly flat, almost dead level. This flat, which extends into the eastern half of Richmond, was originally one of the muddiest settlements in Australia. So, like the Rocks, it was left to the poor and unfortunate. Huts, and even tents, arose on pocket-handkerchief subdivisions in a maze of muddy alleys. Unlike other inner suburbs, Collingwood was never noted much for mansions or charming two-storey terrace houses.

All this is not to say that the shaping of the urban environment is the result of impersonal, subsocial forces. Impersonal forces preoccupied the school of urban studies at the University of Chicago in the 1920s, but there has since been a reaction against this view. Recent writings on comparative urban development have stressed that land-use and settlement patterns in a particular community are influenced by that community's set of values—that is, by its notions about what constitutes rational land-use. These values may vary from community to community. As sociologist Jean Martin says in an article about suburbia in Adelaide, South Australia:

> The physical environment determines the distribution of population and institutions only in that it sets limits to the kind of cultural values that can be developed or maintained, and, within these limits, provides scope for the expression of these values in certain ways but not in others.[7]

To correct the conventional generalizations about concentric zones and urban decay, a study of inner-suburban development must take into account two kinds of environment—the kind found in Fitzroy and western Richmond and the kind found in Collingwood and eastern Richmond. There are two ways of doing this. Either we can take Richmond as a case study (and examine the difference between the hill in the west and the flat in the east) or we can take Fitzroy and Collingwood as a case study (and examine the difference between the hill in Fitzroy and the flat in Collingwood). This book follows the second course; the division into two

8

municipalities enables a more ready comparison of source materials. Therefore many statements made about Fitzroy and Collingwood in this book are relevant also to western Richmond and eastern Richmond respectively. Readers may also recognize parallels with neighbourhoods in other towns and cities. In studying Collingwood and Fitzroy, we encounter many problems that have at some time bothered communities throughout Australia. Of the two suburbs, Collingwood has had a greater share of problems. It was indeed Melbourne's multi-problem suburb. Therefore this book will focus on Collingwood, while making frequent comparisons with Fitzroy.

Collingwood makes an ideal case study in the origins of pollution. In 1852 this suburb began a long, painful lesson in the logic of urban development. If thousands of people settle in a compact area, they require enormous quantities of water, food, fuel, durable goods and packaging, as well as the construction materials (timber, bricks, iron) needed to build the town itself. But people do not really 'consume' these things. We merely change their form, and in the process produce an enormous output of sewage, garbage, junk, smoke, dust, smells and rubble. Impulsively we discard this refuse on the ground or in water or into the air in the hope that it will be absorbed, diluted, invisible and forgotten. In Collingwood, largely because of the topography, the sink became choked earlier than it did elsewhere. This community was soon wading in its own muck. In addition, Collingwood became a cesspool for refuse which gravitated from higher areas. This refuse included not only sewage and rubbish, but also people—a continuing influx of the unwanted poor in search of cheap shelter. (The story of sanitation and pollution is introduced in chapters 3 and 4 and told fully in chapters 5 to 8.)

A study of Collingwood and its neighbours helps us to understand some of the processes of suburbanization in Australia. In the early City of Melbourne the initiative in forming civic policy was taken by city businessmen. In the first suburbs the initiative was taken by smaller, local businessmen. These included builders, contractors, publicans, grocers, bakers, butchers, bootmakers and other self-employed artisans, as well as landlords with a cottage to let or a yard to subdivide. About 1855, Collingwood's businessmen were alarmed by a decline in local land values, rents and business and by the district's poor reputation. In order to bring about improvements, it would be necessary to bring Collingwood under a system of municipal government. But this would mean municipal taxation on local property. The businessmen wished to minimize this taxation and to maximize returns. Therefore they shrewdly avoided being absorbed into the existing City of Melbourne. Melbourne City Council, they realized, was committed to the improvement of the heart of the city—a rival business district. Instead, the Collingwood businessmen managed to have their district declared an independent municipality—the third municipality established in Victoria (after Melbourne and Geelong). One by one, other suburban districts did likewise—South Melbourne, Richmond, Fitzroy and so on. Thus the growing metropolis became fragmented into the dozens of separate local-government areas that exist today.

This fragmentation created many problems of metropolitan sanitation. For thirty years after 1855, the suburban councils failed to combine with the City of Melbourne in providing money for the proper disposal of sewage. The metropolis proudly known as 'marvellous Melbourne' became derided as 'marvellous Smelbourne'. In the late 1880s the suburbs finally agreed to co-operate in establishing the Melbourne and Metropolitan Board of Works but only after this was shown to be, from the suburban viewpoint, a reasonable business proposition.

However, the businessmen within a suburb were by no means united. Because they were spaced out along a number of thoroughfares, they split into factions with rival plans for fostering local prosperity. This is why they continually squabbled over the location of roads, bridges, drainage, municipal buildings, tramways and railways. (These suburban processes are analysed in chapters 3, 4 and 9.)

The Collingwood experience also illuminates the processes of Australia's industrialization. Early capital investment in Collingwood was absorbed in constructing houses, hotels, shops and streets rather than factories. Long before factories became typical there, the small local businessmen tended to regard streets as vast assembly lines for mass-producing customers and tenants. Initial growth depended upon rapid population increase. For twenty years after 1855, Collingwood's population was the largest of all Melbourne's suburban municipalities and was among the largest in Australia—comparable with the gold town, Bendigo, and indeed at times not much smaller than Hobart or Brisbane. This meant that Collingwood had a vast supply of cheap labour—unskilled workers, unemployed craftsmen and, increasingly, adolescents and women. But at first industry was not ready for them. In the 1860s a demand for factory development arose in Collingwood and Richmond (see chapters 6 and 7). This demand had widespread support from small businessmen seeking a more prosperous local economy and another source of municipal revenue, from workers seeking more employment opportunities, from industrialists or would-be industrialists interested in developing capital, and from well-meaning people who believed that industry would be 'good' for the district. Collingwood and Richmond became the headquarters of the Protectionist movement, agitating for tariffs to protect colonial industry against foreign imports. Thus the district played a significant role in the development of Australian industry. Indeed the Collingwood-Richmond district was envisaged as the future Manchester of the southern hemisphere, with the River Yarra as its ship canal.

Like Sydney's Botany area, nineteenth-century Collingwood and Richmond specialized in noxious industries. These were mostly concerned with animal products—slaughter yards, tanneries, soap and candle works, and works for cleaning sheepskins and wool. There were also breweries, brickworks and a night-soil trade. All these contributed to the pollution of the environment. In the nineteenth century, legal restrictions on pollution were inadequate and were not properly enforced. Local businessmen, including the municipal councillors, usually regarded public health matters in business terms. To foster local prosperity, they permitted industry to use the River Yarra as a sewer, and even tried through parliament to make this legal. Yarra pollution, they said, was an economic necessity. This 'business view' of civic development was common in Australian towns in the nineteenth century—and still is today.

For the benefit of readers outside Melbourne, I have been relating Collingwood in this chapter to other places outside Melbourne, but it is impossible to find any satisfactory counterpart. Collingwood and the Rocks, for example, both had a bad start, but for different reasons, and their later roles diverged. For one thing, Collingwood was more suburban. Its location in relation to the central business district was probably more comparable with Sydney's Waterloo-Alexandria area, but industrially Collingwood also performed some of the functions of Botany. Many readers may recognize parallels between Collingwood and some of the inner areas in London's low-lying Lea Valley: Bethnal Green, Poplar and Stepney. The Commissioners under the Poor Law of 1834 spoke about the 'unhealthy' undrained marshes of Bethnal Green, and later there was similar talk in Melbourne about the unhealthy undrained marshes of Collingwood. Other readers may think the impact of gold immigrants on Collingwood in the 1850s resembles in some ways the impact of poor Irish immigrants on the slums of Boston and New York about 1847, as described by Cecil Woodham-Smith in *The Great Hunger* (1962). But for every similarity there are significant differences. Collingwood was never as squalid as poor neighbourhoods abroad. Its dwellings were chiefly single-storey, and were generally occupied by one family, often by the owners. It was not a major centre of vice and crime. Melbourne's main brothels, for example, developed around Little Lonsdale Street in the central business district, and when they expanded it was chiefly into suburbs that were falling from gentility—Fitzroy and St Kilda. Collingwood was basically a community of low-paid workers.

Although housing and sanitation were bad, it would be misleading to speak of Collingwood as a 'slum'. A dictionary defines a slum as 'a dirty crowded poor district in a town', but the word is lacking in precision. H. J. Dyos, the English writer on urbanization, says:

> Like poverty itself, slums have always been . . . relative things, both in terms of neighbouring affluence and in terms of what is intolerable or accepted by those living in or near them. Such a term has no fixity . . . It is not now possible to invent a satisfactory definition of a slum in the nineteenth century.[8]

Or, as the American sociologist and planner Herbert J. Gans says (*People and Plans*, 1968): 'The term "slum" is an evaluative, not an empirical one.' Today urban-redevelopment and road-building authorities are prone to apply the term 'slum' to any building that stands in their way. In line with Jane Jacobs (*The Death and Life of Great American Cities*, 1961), it is probably wiser to think of Collingwood as an area of low-cost housing rather than of slums.

For many people, Collingwood has been a satisfactory place to live. Apart from the low-cost housing, there was local employment. Whereas middle-class suburbs tend to be dormitories for people employed in the central business district or elsewhere, Collingwood people generally worked together. Although the focus of this book is the shaping of the environment, it must be remembered that Collingwood was a community, and that it always commanded a greater degree of commitment from its residents than most other Melbourne suburbs did. This has been evidenced by the enormous local support for the Collingwood football team in the Victorian Football League. Families stayed in Collingwood for generations, often by choice as much as necessity. Collingwood was like this at least until World War II. Since then, many former residents have been dispersed and have been replaced by European migrants. Throughout Australia today there are people who will fiercely defend Collingwood as a place where they enjoyed life.

The story of Melbourne's inner suburbs begins in 1838, when the township on the River Yarra was three years old. The authorities in Sydney decided to auction a tract of Crown land adjoining Melbourne. The land was cut into eighty-eight portions, each about twenty-five acres. Those portions numbered from 1 to 47, to the east of Melbourne, later became the municipality of Richmond. The remaining forty-one portions to the north, numbered from 48 to 88, became known colloquially as the 'district of Collingwood' and were represented jointly in Victoria's first parliaments as the 'electorate of Collingwood' but administratively they have always been divided into two local government areas. The twelve portions west of Smith Street, nearest to Melbourne, were originally part of the City of Melbourne, but they severed from Melbourne in 1858 to become the municipality of Fitzroy. Colloquially, Fitzroy continued to be known throughout the 1860s as 'upper Collingwood' or 'Collingwood west'. Meanwhile, the twenty-nine portions east of Smith Street became known as 'East' Collingwood but they were never within the City of Melbourne, a fact which proved to be of great significance in the development of Collingwood and of the metropolis. Administratively, East Collingwood was a no-man's land until 1855. In that year it became the 'municipality of East Collingwood'. In 1873 it officially dropped the prefix 'East', for by this time Fitzroy no longer wished to be associated with the name of Collingwood and was glad to abandon it to its eastern neighbour.

In England, 'Collingwood' had been the name of a celebrated aristocrat. In Victoria, as a place name, it ended up at the bottom of the social scale—an interesting transformation.

This brings us to the question of topography. Travelling east from Melbourne along Victoria Parade, one finds several sharp changes. First, there is a hill, known as Melbourne's Eastern Hill.

The hill's crest, about three-quarters of a mile from Melbourne's General Post Office, lies in southern Fitzroy, in Portions 48, 49, 50 and 51. When one reaches East Collingwood at Smith Street (about a mile from the G.P.O.), the scene changes rather abruptly. There is a steep slope down Portion 52 to Portion 53, but this is short—only about two hundred yards. Most of Collingwood, the mile or so from Portion 53 to the Yarra, is a plain, known colloquially as Collingwood Flat. The Flat is the result of prehistoric flows of basalt from volcanic activity north of Melbourne. The basalt flows partially filled the ancestral valley of the Merri Creek (a tributary of the Yarra), and flowed down the ancestral valley of the Yarra from about a mile above Collingwood (near the present site of Fairfield) to Spencer Street, Melbourne. The Yarra was forced to the eastern fringe of the basalt, cutting a fresh winding valley through today's Studley Park. The basalt covered the pre-existing alluvial gravels, sands and clays in the old valleys, but low hills such as the Eastern Hill in Fitzroy protrude through the basalt. Until the 1840s the region was wooded, especially the Hill. The Flat, however, was heavily encumbered with boulders; further-more it was the receptacle for storm-water from the Hill and the Slope, as well as from the Crown lands of North Fitzroy and Clifton Hill. The water flowed through a swamp in Portions 85 and 86; it then spread across the Flat to a creek and swamp in Portions 65 and 66, adjoining the Yarra. These three regions—southern Fitzroy's Hill, the East Collingwood Slope and the East Collingwood Flat—differ in their urban development from about 1850.

Unlike some other settlements in Victoria, Fitzroy and East Collingwood were not originally designed as urban areas. The government's pre-auction survey created only paddocks. The ground-plan adopted was the conventional gridiron—straight boundaries and uniform distances, easily surveyed and transacted. At the auctions, held in Sydney, the land went in quite large parcels: one purchaser obtained 9 portions (totalling 230 acres), two purchasers obtained 4 portions (100 acres) each; six obtained 2 portions each; and twelve obtained 1 each. During the 1840s some portions changed hands. In the 1840s and early 1850s the biggest landowners were quite substantial men, including pastoral-ists (J. D. L. Campbell, Charles Nicholson, Benjamin Baxter, Charles Hutton, John Orr, John Dight), merchants (John Hodg-son, George Ward Cole, J. T. Hughes and J. Hosking), solicitors (John Matthew Smith, J. W. Thurlow, R. H. Way, T. B. Payne),

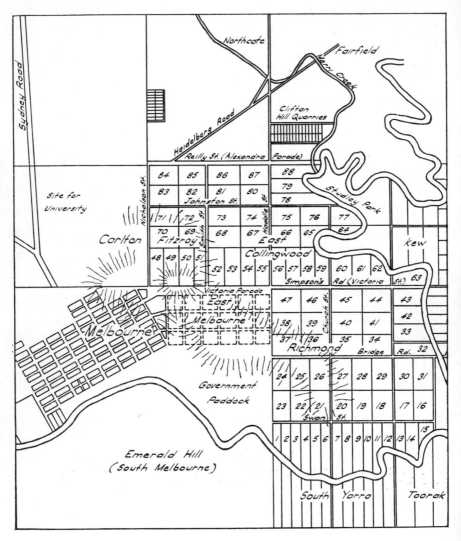

Melbourne and environs as sold by the Crown in the 1830s.

land agents (J. M. Holloway, W. C. Henley), a ship owner (J. T. E. Flint), an army officer (P. L. Campbell) and a clergyman (George Otter). Two of these—J. D. L. Campbell and T. B. Payne—were among the wealthiest men in Victoria; several—Hodgson, Thurlow, Hughes and Hosking—over-reached themselves and experienced insolvency.

From 1838 until today, the designing of Fitzroy and East Collingwood has been the work of countless amateurs. First the owner of a Crown portion would run some streets through according to his own whims and would sell the new frontages, probably in large parcels; then his successors repeated the process on a diminishing scale. At each stage, the subdivider sold to men who were poorer than himself. The gridiron ground-plan was ideal for speculation. Its standardization facilitated a maximum number of building allotments, all allotments oblong, all allotments fronting on to a thoroughfare, all prices measured in frontage feet. The procedure was simple enough for any speculator, auctioneer, solicitor, builder, apprentice or office boy. That is why all streets in Fitzroy and East Collingwood south of Reilly Street run at right-angles—north-south, east-west—except for several where curves were necessary to standardize riverside allotments.

The pattern of subdivision of the forty-one Crown portions in Fitzroy and East Collingwood may be traced by sifting through certain documents at the Victorian Titles Office—official search notes made at a relatively late stage when various properties were being changed from the general-law system of land registration to the current Torrens system. From these notes, it is possible to distinguish six main stages in the subdividing process, as shown in the accompanying diagrams.

Stage 1, of course, is the government's sale of 1838–9. Stage 2 began in 1839 on the Hill. There, Benjamin Baxter intersected his field (Portion 49) with a neat crossroad pattern (Gertrude Street and Brunswick Street) and began disposing of the new frontages. The new intersection was situated about two hundred yards beyond the crest of the Hill; being protected from Melbourne's dust, mud and noise, it was a more attractive site than Melbourne itself. A village—called at first Newtown but more commonly Collingwood West—developed there, apparently stimulated by the government's slowness in doling out land in Melbourne proper before 1840. The first settlers were 'gentlemen' from Melbourne.

In Stage 3, the owner of Portion 70, R. S. Webb, continued Brunswick Street northward into his land, creating further market-

17

c

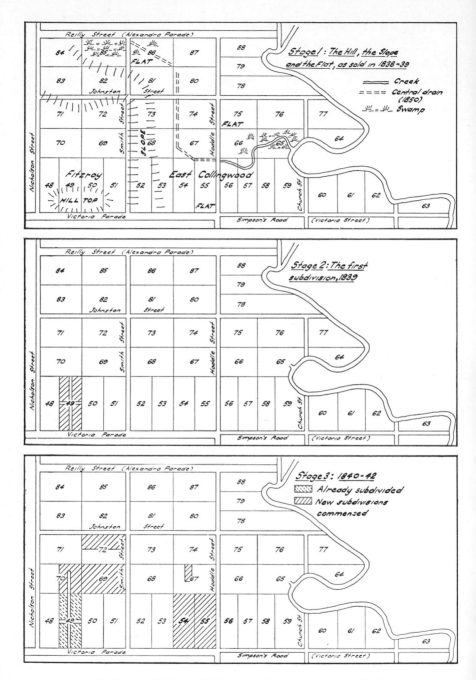

Stages in the subdivision of Fitzroy and East Collingwood, 1838–42.

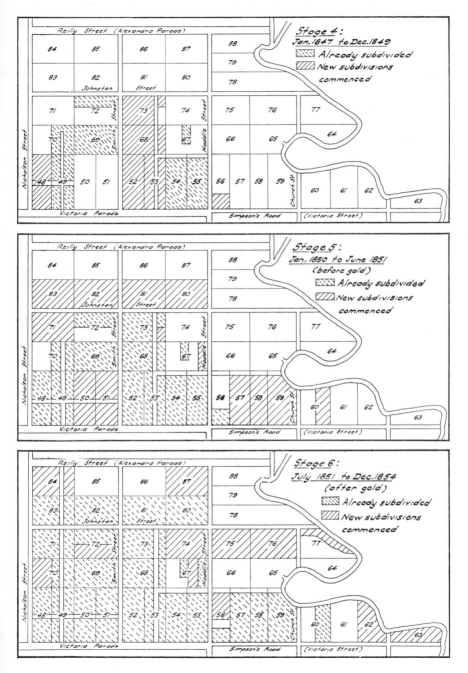

Stages in the subdivision of Fitzroy and East Collingwood, 1847–54.

able frontages. Downhill from Newtown, several other portions (Nos. 69 and 72 to the north and Nos. 54, 55 and 67 on the East Collingwood Flat) were subdivided, chiefly by John Hodgson, but, being more remote and less elevated, these portions were less valuable than Portion 49. Judging from Titles Office records, the typical purchaser at these sales of 1839–42 acquired several allotments, and disposed of them singly during the 1840s and 1850s.

Stage 4 began on the Hill in the late 1840s with Gertrude Street being extended to create new frontages in Portion 48. Meanwhile, on the Slope, Captain Charles Hutton subdivided Portions 52, 53 and 68, creating a new north-south axis, Wellington Street, and the Reverend George Otter continued this street into his Portion 73. These subdivisions illustrate a basic feature of Fitzroy and East Collingwood: the district is really a mosaic of several dozen different bits of amateur urban design. The original subdivider of each Crown portion would draw up a street plan with little, if any, reference to the layout being adopted in neighbouring portions. As well as creating Wellington Street, Hutton and Otter each created several shorter streets, but they did not co-ordinate these; Hutton's seem to be oriented chiefly north-south, and Otter's east-west. Nor did they align their streets with those already laid out in Portions 69, 72, 54 or 55, or with those about to be laid out in Portions 50 and 51. When subdividers extended Gertrude Street through Portions 50 and 51 to Smith Street in 1850 (Stage 5), it was blocked there by Charles Hutton's different planning logic; removing such bottlenecks became a major theme in the local politics of the 1850s and 1860s. The speculator was credited with the immediate profits resulting from his operations; the long-term losses accrued to the residents and to the public purse.

At the end of 1849, most portions in Fitzroy and East Collingwood were still unsubdivided, although, according to the Titles Office, only seven still had their original owners. For example, when Hughes and Hosking became insolvent in 1848, four portions still held by them north of Johnston Street (Nos. 80 to 83) passed to the Bank of Australasia until subdivided in 1850. As shown in our diagram for Stage 5, these subdivisions were faulty in failing to allow for the continuation northward of Brunswick Street or Wellington Street—another burning issue for the 1850s and 1860s.

By 1850 a building boom was developing in Fitzroy. The census of 1851 shows 3,449 people and 678 houses there. According to the Melbourne daily newspaper, the *Argus*, the newcomers now included 'working men' as well as 'gentlemen' and tensions developed between these two groups. The gentlemen, being concentrated on the Hill, were high and dry and virtually in Melbourne proper. Their two major streets (Gertrude Street and Brunswick Street) were kept in repair by Melbourne City Council. This was not surprising, since gentlemen were well represented on the Council. The working men, however, were scattered down the slopes to the north. Vainly they sought City Council funds to untangle and construct their maze of muddy alleys. During a Melbourne City Council election campaign in 1850, a spokesman for the working men summed up the situation in Fitzroy thus:

> The struggle is one of right against might—of the district proper against the aristocracy of Brunswick Street . . . One candidate . . . has called the district's people a set of ragamuffins but I hope, although we are most of us humble, we are as good and as honest and, though workingmen, as intelligent as those who call us ragamuffins.[1]

These tensions in Fitzroy, which can be indicated only briefly here, represent one of the earliest stages in a long train of events that culminated in the fragmentation of the original municipality of Melbourne. The 'working men' of 1850 succeeded in having Fitzroy constituted as a separate ward, although still within the City of Melbourne. (Previously Fitzroy had been part of a larger ward, which also included Carlton.) After 1850, the Melbourne City Council's procrastination over street works in the Fitzroy ward finally caused Fitzroy to break away as a separate municipality in 1858. Interestingly, a comparable conflict of interests began in the mid-1850s in East Collingwood between the Slope and the Flat, and this will be analysed in later chapters. Something similar also occurred in Richmond.

In terms of launchings, the peak year for new subdivisions in Fitzroy and East Collingwood was 1850, when eight portions were opened up. In terms of the component parts, the rate of individual dealings registered at the Titles Office was steady during 1850 and 1851, and increased markedly to a peak in 1852–3, the years of gold immigration. For example, Charles Nicholson's subdivision of Portions 57–59 on the Flat was first advertised in April 1851 (on the eve of the gold discovery); his dealings began four months later and continued until 1870.

The process of further subdivision—i.e., subdividing land that has already been subdivided—is illustrated by the case of John Hodgson. As well as owning complete Crown portions (Portions 69, 54, 55, 67), he also bought in 1849 two smaller slices. One (the southern end of Portion 56) he subdivided immediately; the other (the south-eastern corner of Portion 73) he subdivided in March 1851 and sold in thirty pieces, mainly 1852–3. However, many of the plots created in the 1850s, particularly on the Flat, remained vacant and unfenced for up to twenty years.

Despite the changes in land ownership, East Collingwood was still desolate in 1851, particularly on the Flat. The buildings comprised chiefly a few isolated cottages and wayside inns and a glass factory. Along the Yarra were seven homes of pastoral pioneers of the 1840s. East Collingwood's boom in population and building began when gold immigrants overflowed from Melbourne in mid-1852. In mid-1851 the construction of John Hodgson's bluestone Studley Arms Hotel in Wellington Street was interrupted by the rush to the goldfields; in mid-1852 the hotel was enlarged to accommodate gold immigrants.

Gold immigration intensified an upward trend in land values that appears in Titles Office records from 1839 and more particularly from 1849. In 1839 the Crown portions brought about £17 an acre on the riverside (Portion 63) or about £5 on the Flat; by 1852–4 Portion 63 (cut into four paddocks) changed hands for £193 an acre, and three unsubdivided portions on the Flat brought £41 an acre (Portion 87), £62 10s an acre (Portion 86) and even £356 an acre (Portion 74). During the gold immigration, as shown in our diagram for Stage 6, new subdivisions were launched even in the most remote areas of the Flat. Old subdivisions were cut up further.

An examination of auction advertisements for East Collingwood in the *Argus* in 1851–8 reveals that some subdividers sought to exploit the Flat's proximity to 'the beautiful River Yarra' and to the riverside pastoral homesteads. An advertisement for 'the new township of Abbotsford' in Portions 76 and 77 observed that 'a river in its serpentine wanderings carries with it health, prosperity and abundance', and announced that the first allotments offered would be riverside ones in St Hellier's Street in Portion 77: 'The allotments all along this terrace discover Gardens of Delight, where woods and vallies, orchards and meadows, present a thousand beauties &c.' This claim became less true as the natural beauties were replaced by buildings—e.g. (by 1858) the Melbourne Laundry. In another advertisement, Grosvenor Street in Portion 61 was said to be 'about ten minutes walk to Parliament House . . . near the residence of the Hon. the Speaker (Sir Francis Murphy) . . . bounded on one side by Mr Norton's Beautiful Garden.' The distance referred to is really a mile and a half, necessitating a ten-minute

Webb's Paddock (Portion 70) Fitzroy, in the 1840s. This eventually became one of the most densely populated parts of Melbourne.

sprint. In the twentieth century this street became overshadowed by the Abbotsford Brewery, the Kodak film factory and the Phoenix biscuit factory. Murphy's residence, Mayfield, was demolished in 1962 after being bought by a clothing manufacturing company.

Most advertisements stressed the cheapness of the land—from 3s 6d to 10s a foot in the early 1850s. Portion 87, for example, was subdivided in 1852 at 5s a foot, or £6 5s for a whole 25-ft frontage. And terms were easy: in Portion 74 in 1853, they were one-half or one-third cash, and the remainder at six and thirteen months. The Flat, said Charles Nicholson's advertisements, was an opportunity for recent immigrants to become freeholders. (If a man could not obtain a hundred acres in the squatters' countryside, he could at least obtain one-sixth of an acre, it seemed, on the fringe of the city.)

Even before the gold discovery, advertisements pointed out that East Collingwood, being beyond the Melbourne City boundary, was exempt from the Building Act that discouraged small or wooden houses. During the gold immigration, advertisements stressed that East Collingwood, being on land already alienated from the Crown, was ideal for 'those who, unable to obtain lodgings, may wish to pitch tents where the Crown Lands Commissioner dare not molest them'. A similar point was made in a newspaper editorial. 'We cannot build fast enough with brick or stone', said the *Argus*. 'The only alternative appears to be . . . the immediate erection of wooden buildings . . . just outside the boundaries indicated by the Building Act.'[2] So in 1852 a community sprang up at East Collingwood within a few months. By 1854 East Collingwood was overtaking Fitzroy in both population (about 9,000 each) and houses (about 2,000 each); thereafter, as shown in Table 1, East Collingwood kept the lead. In the censuses of 1857, 1861 and 1871 East Collingwood was Melbourne's most populous suburb.

The rate of dwelling construction can be seen by comparing survey plans drafted in 1853, 1856 and 1858 by Clement Hodgkinson, a surveyor in the Victorian Surveyor-General's Office. These plans, some of which are preserved in the Victorian Lands Department, were intended to show all buildings. The first survey was commissioned late in 1852 by a select committee of the Legislative Council, which was inquiring into water supply and sewerage for Melbourne. The survey, which began relatively early in the period of gold immigration, covered Melbourne proper, East Melbourne, Fitzroy, East Collingwood and Richmond. In this plan, East Col-

TABLE 1

Population and dwellings, East Collingwood and Fitzroy,
1851–91

Year	Population		Dwellings	
	E. C'wood	Fitzroy	E. C'wood	Fitzroy
1851	?	3,449	?	678
1854	8,738	9,172	?	?
1857	10,786	10,609	2,619	2,220
1861	12,653	11,807	3,478	2,703
1871	18,598	15,547	4,257	3,256
1881	23,829	22,742	5,085	4,612
1891	35,070	32,452	7,673	6,591

lingwood's building development is shown as being chiefly on the Slope, and most of those buildings are surrounded by vacant allotments. The Flat is merely dotted with buildings here and there. (At this stage, most streets on the Flat existed only on paper.)

The 1856 plan was drafted at the request of the East Collingwood municipal council soon after the council was established. This shows a big change since 1853. On the Slope, almost every allotment is built on. The Flat, while still mostly vacant, has several houses in each 'street'.

In the late 1850s about half of East Collingwood's population lived on the Slope (west of Wellington Street) and half on the Flat. The change is summed up in 1855 in a newspaper article about the glass factory, in Portion 54:

> Some few years ago the old Glasshouse at Collingwood stood alone in the centre of the swamp, and the few who ventured near the spot were looked upon after their return as people who had performed a somewhat perilous journey . . . Now however . . . the old Glasshouse is no longer in the country, and the city omnibuses travel regularly to within a few minutes' walk of the spot. So great are the changes effected, and so rapid has been the progress of building, that people with old associations about them—for they seem old if only dating six years ago—begin to look upon such buildings as interesting antiquities.[3]

These basic circumstances of East Collingwood—its depressed topography, its commercialized ground plan, its location beyond the city boundary, and its exemption from the city building regulations—were to limit the kind of visual and social environment that could develop there.

Regarding the visual environment, it is interesting to assess trends in the shaping of East Collingwood's living space—its streets and private allotments. This may be done by examining ground-plans which were prepared by the major subdividers at auction time. Plans for hundreds of Melbourne land auctions are preserved in a collection of real-estate papers at the State Library of Victoria. In addition, a few East Collingwood plans are preserved at the Collingwood City Engineer's Office. From these and other sources including the Titles Office, it is possible to construct a table (Table 2) showing typical measurements of some original sub-divisions.

TABLE 2

Measurements in some portions when first subdivided

Year first subdivided	Crown portion	Width of earliest streets (ft)	Typical original frontage (ft)	Typical original depth (ft)
1841	Nos. 54, 55	33	91	120
1848	No. 73	66	?	?
1849	Nos. 52, 53	66	?	?
1850	No. 80	52	66	100
1850	No. 81	52	33	100
1851	Nos. 57, 58, 59	66	?	?
1852	No. 87	66	25	82
1852	No. 75	33	?	?
1853	No. 76	33	33	97
1853	No. 74	47	26	70
1858	No. 61	40	40	90
1869	No. 86	50	26	80
1873	No. 67	33	25	63
1880	Nos. 78, 79, 88	66	33	132
1885	No. 60	40	33	95

As Table 2 shows, street space was more generously provided in portions subdivided before 1851 than after. All portions subdivided in 1848–51 were intersected with thoroughfares 66 ft wide or 52 ft wide. The only pre-1851 pattern of narrow thoroughfares was that of John Hodgson in Portions 54 and 55—and this was in 1841 when such grassy country lanes carried little traffic. In 1852–8 only one portion was laid out with 66 ft thoroughfares; half a dozen other portions were given widths of 47 ft, 40 ft, or, more typically, 33 ft. The changing fashion in widths is seen in two subdivisions initiated by T. B. Payne two years apart—streets 52 ft wide in Portions 80 and 81 in 1850 and 33 ft wide in Portion 75 in 1852. The comments just made refer, of course, only to the very earliest streets on each portion. As other men subdivided further, streets of 30 ft width appeared: John Hodgson was responsible for at least four of these in 1849–52.

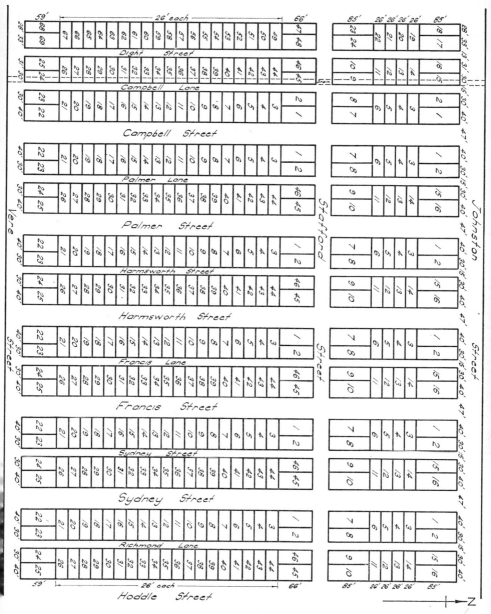

An auctioneer's plan of subdivision for Portion 74, 1853; it shows 400 building plots on 26 acres. This typical commercial ground-plan shows how the flat ground facilitated standardization.

After 1851, streets (or, rather, alleys) of 20 to 25 ft began to appear. At first these were mostly off, or near, the east side of Wellington Street in Portions 68 and 53; three appear there in Hodgkinson's survey of 1853, another six in that of 1856. These alleys were originally intended as rights-of-way, giving access to stables and the like at the rear of properties, but in the early 1850s the alleys received names (e.g., Glasshouse Road), and the frontages thus created were sold or leased. Thus, when East Collingwood Council was established in 1855, most of the named streets in today's Collingwood were already in existence. The council counted ninety-seven named streets, amounting to 25 miles. Of these, forty-three streets (or 45 per cent) were between 20 ft and 33 ft wide. The council announced that it would prefer future new streets to be 40 ft wide, and the Central Board of Health in 1887 recommended the government to set a minimum of 66 ft, but these gestures came too late for Collingwood. In addition to named streets or alleys, there also developed by the 1880s many un-named rights-of-way, or back lanes, of about 10 ft or less, often with a dead end. These had no frontage worth selling, but the stables and shacks along them eventually harboured tenants, especially during economic depressions.

Like the public space of the streets, the space of private allotments tended to dwindle, too. As shown in Table 2, subdivisions with 33-ft frontages were auctioned in East Collingwood by 1850. After 1851, auctions of 26-ft frontages became common. Furthermore (and this is not shown in the table) allotments created in, say, 1850 tended to be cut in half in 1860, 1870, or 1880. For example, in swampy Portion 80, 66-ft frontages created (but unsold) in 1850 became 33-ft frontages (and sold) after drainage improvements there in 1869. With depths as small as 63 ft (see Table 2) or even less, tiny backyards were inevitable.

An effective way to examine East Collingwood is to compare it with Fitzroy, using data from the census reports of 1851, 1854, 1857, 1861, 1871, 1881, and 1891. According to these, the two places were consistently similar in two respects—in national origin and in religion (except that Fitzroy had somewhat more Jews and East Collingwood had somewhat more Primitive Methodists). But in several other respects there were significant differences.

One difference was in buildings. As shown in Tables 3 and 4, Fitzroy's houses were generally stone or brick (63 per cent in 1851, 64 per cent in 1861), with about four rooms. The larger houses,

TABLE 3

Material of dwellings in East Collingwood and Fitzroy, 1857–91

Material	1857 no.	%	1861 no.	%	1871 no.	%	1881 no.	%	1891 no.	%
	East Collingwood									
Brick or stone	486	19	861	24	1,265	30	2,037	40	3,904	51
Wood, iron, etc.	2,101	80	2,529	74	2,822	66	2,961	58	3,641	47
Not stated	32	1	88	2	170	4	87	2	128	2
Total	2,619		3,478		4,257		5,085		7,673	
	Fitzroy									
Brick or stone	?		1,739	64	2,401	74	3,605	78	5,477	83
Wood, iron, etc.	?		749	28	802	24	955	21	936	14
Not stated	?		215	8	53	2	52	1	178	3
Total	2,220		2,703		3,256		4,612		6,591	

The census of 1851 provides data on Fitzroy only: stone or brick, 63 per cent; wooden, 37 per cent.

TABLE 4

Size of dwellings in East Collingwood and Fitzroy, 1857–91

No. of rooms	1857 no.	%	1861 no.	%	1871 no.	%	1881 no.	%	1891 no.	%
	East Collingwood									
7 or more	50	2	93	3	184	4	326	6	662	8
5 or 6	147	6	263	8	498	12	917	18		
3 or 4	962	36	1,568	45	2,403	56	3,086	61 } 6,493	85
1 or 2	1,437	55	1,448	41	920	22	553	11	361	5
Not stated	23	1	106	3	252	6	203	4	157	2
Total	2,619		3,478		4,257		5,085		7,673	
	Fitzroy									
7 or more	150	7	302	11	471	14	727	16	1,289	20
5 or 6	319	14	419	16	658	20	1,126	24		
3 or 4	981	44	1,156	42	1,588	49	2,348	51 } 4,807	73
1 or 2	722	33	593	22	455	14	324	7	253	3
Not stated	48	2	233	9	84	3	87	2	242	4
Total	2,220		2,703		3,256		4,612		6,591	

particularly in the south, were commonly double-storeyed. East Collingwood's houses, however, were generally wooden (80 per cent in 1857), with only one or two rooms. A double-storeyed house was rare in East Collingwood. The contrast between solid Fitzroy and flimsy East Collingwood is evident in Hodgkinson's surveys, which show, by colouring or shading, the materials of each building.

Housing on the Flat in 1853 is recalled in the Collingwood-Fitzroy *Observer* in 1865:

> Well do we remember, in those days of thigh boots—when to venture out after dark in slushy weather was no joke—the motley collection of tin and packing-case shanties, dignified with the name of habitations, that were sparsely dotted through the chaos of crabholes and boulders.[4]

Some houses had 'partitions formed of calico, covered by a cheap tawdry paper, flapping backwards and forwards in every breeze, here and there disreputably hanging down'. One reason for some of this inferior housing was that some speculators (e.g., W. C. Henley in Portions 54 and 55) provided building allotments for leasing, not for sale. Consequently settlers erected 'temporary' dwellings, which, after the original leases expired, became permanent eyesores.

The few substantial buildings were chiefly hotels. According to Hodgkinson's 1856 survey, the western half of East Collingwood (i.e., between Smith Street and Hoddle Street, comprising all the Slope and part of the Flat) had nineteen well-established hotels as well as many lesser grog-shops, compared with only two churches (Independent and Wesleyan) and a church school (Anglican).

Another contrast between East Collingwood and Fitzroy appears in the census data on occupations. Even at a glance, one notices that Fitzroy consistently scored highly in certain occupations, usually regarded as being socially superior, while East Collingwood scored highly in others, usually socially inferior. It is possible to assess these differences less impressionistically by re-shuffling the dozens of occupational categories for males and sorting them for our purposes into, say, four main groupings or ranks, corresponding approximately (within the limitations of the census categories) to common notions about the stratification of society:[5]

> Rank A: Professionals, merchants and gentlemen.
> Rank B: Shopkeepers and lesser professionals.
> Rank C: Clerks, artisans and carriers.
> Rank D: Labourers.

The occupations, re-arranged, are listed fully in Table 5. If we obtain totals for the number of men falling within each of our ranks and convert these to percentages, the result for 1854 is:

	E. C'wood %	Fitzroy %
Rank A:	8	14
Rank B:	17	20
Rank C:	56	53
Rank D:	19	13

Assessed thus, Fitzroy was undoubtedly 'superior'. This finding is confirmed by the census reports of 1857 and 1861 and later. For 1861 our percentages are:

	E. C'wood %	Fitzroy %
Rank A:	3	6
Rank B:	20	24
Rank C:	60	57
Rank D:	17	13

From details shown in Table 5, it will be seen that in 1854 Fitzroy easily surpassed East Collingwood in every occupation in our Rank A and in almost every occupation in Rank B (excepting food traders, shopkeepers and hawkers). In Rank C the two municipalities were fairly evenly matched, the most striking difference being that East Collingwood had more members of the building trades. In Rank D East Collingwood excelled in most categories (the largest one being labourers), although Fitzroy had more unemployed. In the 1861 census, the relationship between the two municipalities remained substantially as in 1854. In both years, then, Fitzroy may be summed up (in terms of the building trades, for example) as the place which had more 'contractors' and East Collingwood as the one which had more carpenters and labourers.

The differences persisted in 1871. Fitzroy, despite its smaller population, outnumbered Collingwood enormously in 1871 in several significant categories: government clerks (44 to 16), clergymen (12 to 5), lawyers (24 to 6), medical men (12 to 1), dentists (4 to 3), chemists (7 to 5), artists (12 to 3), domestic servants (43 to 27), 'capitalists' (10 to 0), merchants (48 to 8), 'gentlemen' (43 to 2). Fitzroy excelled also in tailors, drapers, upholsterers, goldsmiths, jewellers and printers. Collingwood, on the other hand, still outnumbered Fitzroy significantly in builders, carpenters, masons, painters, shoemakers, butchers, noxious trades workers, brickmakers, road labourers and draymen.

Despite their apparent exactness, the census statistics for dwellings and occupations are, of course, only approximate. As pointed out by Sam B. Warner in a study of Boston, U.S.A., heads of households in the nineteenth century often regarded the gatherer of statistics as a potential tax collector and possibly therefore withheld information concerning personal property, its size and its use.[6] There is evidence of a similar tendency in Victoria.

In 1911, for example, Collingwood Council noticed that when its valuer asked householders for the number of occupants the number was commonly understated; the total was 11 per cent lower than the population according to the census, an enormous difference.[7] If the figures given to the valuer were understated, then it is

TABLE 5

A re-arrangement of census data on occupations of males, 1854–61

	1854		1861	
	C'wood	F'roy	C'wood	F'roy
Rank A				
Govt officers, magistrates, etc.	25	57	25	58
Clergy (but not sextons, etc.)	4	17	4	12
Physicians, surgeons, dentists	17	21	14	18
Lawyers	12	31	11	18
Merchants	86	226	12	43
Independent means	86	130	60	78
Total	230	482	126	227
Percentage	8	14	3	6
Rank B				
Municipal officers	3	8	8	7
Chemists, hospital attendants	16	22	13	21
Teachers, architects, journalists	33	63	77	137
Shopkeepers, dealers, hawkers	191	190	136	155
Bankers, accountants, auctioneers	55	120	57	111
Inn-keepers	39	64	54	74
Contractors	72	143	15	25
Squatters, stockholders	2	7	0	7
Food and drink traders	135	106	377	354
Total	546	723	737	891
Percentage	17	20	20	24
Rank C				
Army, navy, police, warders	14	32	18	35
Government workmen and messengers	8	9	15	28
Church assistants (sextons, etc.)	3	0	4	4
Lawyers' clerks and assistants	19	25	23	47
Clerks, shop assistants, storemen	188	275	199	303
Tailors, shoemakers, hatters	112	105	158	176
Domestic servants, cooks, grooms	39	62	64	65
Masons, bricklayers, plasterers			330	184
Smiths, founders			194	126
Carpenters, cabinet- and coach-makers	959	908	562	462
Printers, bookbinders, coopers, etc.			168	192
Tanners, fellmongers, soapboilers			64	18
Gold miners	112	89	21	26
Farmers, market gardeners	14	20	20	33
Carriers, cabmen, wood carters	256	304	297	252
Sailors	37	56	15	23
Miscellaneous	40	49	53	99
Total	1,801	1,934	2,205	2,073
Percentage	56	53	60	57
Rank D				
Quarrymen, road and railway labourers	86	49	83	90
Pastoral labourers, shepherds	6	8	9	3
Farm and garden labourers	24	13	42	26
Porters and messengers	37	27	37	24
Labourers (undefined)	413	264	226	114
Unemployed (chiefly) or no answer	60	110	225	233
Total	626	471	622	490
Percentage	19	13	17	13
Total, all ranks	3,203	3,610	3,690	3,681
Plus: Dependent sons; and hospital patients	1,508	1,371	2,550	2,071
Census total	4,711	4,981	6,240	5,752

reasonable to suspect also the figures given to the census-taker, particularly as municipal officers were often employed as census-takers. In 1857, for example, East Collingwood's first town clerk was the local census-taker; he probably would have obtained assistance or information from the council's rate collector, and municipal rates then were a widely resisted innovation.

There is also a big variation in estimates of the number of dwellings per acre. In 1881 and 1891 the census-taker evidently assumed one dwelling per building allotment. However, in 1937 (when Collingwood's population was not much different from 1891) an unusually exhaustive inspection of backyards revealed poor people living in tiny outhouses more suited as woodsheds or dog-kennels; there were at least 486 dwellings with ceilings of 8 ft or lower, including 162 of 6 ft, 9 of 5 ft, and 2 of 4 ft.[8]

Likewise, in the census of occupations, it is certain that in 1857 and 1861 some persons who described themselves as skilled craftsmen were either unemployed or were currently forced to work at another occupation. And the movement back and forth between 'contractor', 'mason' and 'labourer' is difficult to measure, being geared to slumps and booms. However, these limitations in occupational statistics apply chiefly when an attempt is made to compare, say, East Collingwood in 1854 with East Collingwood in 1857; economic conditions differed in those two years. The limitations are less troublesome if we compare East Collingwood in a certain year with Fitzroy in the same year, for any distorting forces would probably operate in both districts.

East Collingwood's low social status became confirmed after 1854 as Melbourne's housing shortage (and East Collingwood's building boom) began to ease. Stone and brick homes were again available around Melbourne ('that is, for those who can afford to pay', the *Argus* said) and wooden houses became difficult to let. In 1855 the *Argus* reported 'destitution' on Collingwood Flat.[9] Victims were in two categories—the temporarily poor and the permanently poor.

The temporaries were disappointed goldminers and unemployed building artisans. (This problem, said the *Argus*, could be eased if the government and the Melbourne City Council were to use the unemployed on civic works, e.g., street making.) The church-people of the Hill and the Slope, scandalized by imputations that they were allowing the poor to starve, qualified these cases as exaggerated. The churchpeople established, first, a Collingwood Philanthropic Society (which promised, through the Melbourne press, to relieve all pressing cases of destitution) and, later, a Collingwood Free Soup Kitchen (said to be the only one in Melbourne). An unintended consequence was that yet more poor persons, especially the permanently poor, were attracted to Collingwood from other districts.

Prominent among the permanently poor were widows and deserted wives, in search of low rents. Extreme cases cited in the *Argus* included a fatherless family living in a mud-brick hut with an earthen floor and with rags instead of doors and window panes, and a woman who nailed a few boards together as a box to bury her child. Census reports show that females in East Collingwood increased markedly in the late 1850s and significantly outnumbered males thereafter.

TABLE 6

Number of females for every 100 males, 1851–91

	1851	*1854*	*1857*	*1861*	*1871*	*1881*	*1891*
E. C'wood	?	85.48	99	103	106.51	109.38	104.89
Fitzroy	100	84.12	98	105	105.73	107.71	99.08

Another way to measure this phenomenon is to calculate the proportion of dependent sons out of the total male population in the census. In 1854, dependent sons accounted for 32 per cent of all males in East Collingwood and 28 per cent in Fitzroy; in 1861, 41 per cent in East Collingwood and 36 per cent in Fitzroy. Thus, in both categories—females and adolescents—East Collingwood tended to exceed Fitzroy (and, by Victoria-wide standards, even Fitzroy was above average).

This concentration of the underprivileged (by sex or age), with their inferior earning power, provided a pool of cheap labour for the subsequent industrialization of the district. It is also a basic condition of various social problems. Reading court reports in the Collingwood *Observer* throughout the 1860s and 1870s, one is struck by the incidence of social deviance involving women and children. Women were frequently charged with drunkenness, obscene language and other misdemeanours, or were sentenced to lunatic asylums or were found to have committed suicide (usually in the Yarra). Women claimed maintenance from fathers of illegitimate children. Children were charged with being neglected and were dispatched to 'industrial schools'. And after 1870 the district became notorious for its adolescent packs—the larrikins. It would be worthwhile to make a systematic survey of these press reports and of police records, in order to make comparisons between men and women, between one year and another, and between Collingwood and other suburbs. If we count the suicide reports in the *Observer* for 1876, we find seven females and two males—an interesting difference, surely worth further investigation.

To anybody able to afford a more extensive choice, the physical conditions of living on Collingwood Flat were not attractive. For one thing, road communications were deficient, because of poor alignments between subdivisions and because of the absence of a road-making authority. Until 1855 East Collingwood's few main roads—Smith, Wellington, Hoddle, Johnston and Gipps Streets— were the responsibility of Victoria's Central Road Board. They were made roughly with bluestone metal, churned up by cart wheels and hoofs. Any side streets or footpaths were the responsibility of residents. Because of the unmade roads, water carters either refused to supply to people on the Flat or charged them exorbitant prices. Residents of the Flat, said the *Argus*, had to drink 'from their own filthy holes'.[10]

Conditions on the Flat were continually worsened by flooding. The spread of settlement on the Hill and Slope, involving the removal of vegetation and the formation of streets, accelerated the descent of storm-water, which was increasingly charged with household sewage. As East Collingwood (unlike suburbs south of the Yarra) is situated on impervious clay (with its basalt sub-surface), the drainage stagnated on the Flat and had to escape largely by evaporation, making the Flat notorious for 'unhealthy vapours'.

About 1850 an attempt at drainage was made by subdivider John Hodgson who ploughed a ditch, later called the central drain, through Portions 74 and 67. In winter the central drain became a raging gully, in summer a rubbish dump. It became, as the Central Board of Health said in 1860, 'an odious and long-standing nuisance . . . the opprobrium of East Collingwood, as regards the deterioration of health and depreciation of property'.

In 1852 inhabitants petitioned the Legislative Council to drain the Flat. A select committee, inquiring into water supply and sewerage for Melbourne, considered proposals by surveyor Hodgkinson to include Collingwood in a metropolitan system of tubular sewers for house drainage and open channels for storm-water, but nothing was done. In 1854 after the gold-rush subdivisions, Hodgkinson reported:

> The multitude of proprietors of small allotments on the Flat precludes the possibility of constructing the main channels of drainage along the lines that would have been most conformable to the natural configuration of the ground. It will be necessary in order to avoid endless reclamations to confine such drains to crown lands or existing roads.[11]

By the mid-1850s an hour's thunderstorm could create a lake covering two square miles on the Flat, rising two feet to the floors of houses, making the floors and walls damp and mouldy, and sometimes causing the owners to abandon the houses. Census reports show that the proportion of houses uninhabited in East Collingwood, usually about 4 to 6 per cent, rose to 12 per cent after severe flooding in 1861.

Thus, by 1864 (as the Collingwood *Observer* remarked in that year), a whole generation of Melbourne's poor had learned that 'if you go to Collingwood, you can get houses rent-free and soup for nothing'.[12]

THE SUBURBAN FRONTIER

(Collingwood, 1850–60)

The 1850s saw the transformation of Melbourne from a town to a city and from a city to a metropolis. In the new suburban belt, pressure groups arose to campaign for civic improvements (ranging from roads and drainage to water and gas) and for independent local government. East Collingwood, as the first suburb to achieve independence, makes an appropriate case study.

By the end of 1853, after East Collingwood people had experienced their first or second winter there, a general agreement existed that two kinds of improvements were needed—in drainage and in traffic. On one hand, drainage improvement would bring immediate benefit to residents of the Flat and (by attracting more and better residents) would bring long-term benefits to local commerce. 'Much property that is now lying idle', a prominent citizen said, 'would be occupied by a happy and intelligent people. The lovely banks of the Yarra would be peopled by the merchants and shopkeepers of Melbourne.'[1] On the other hand, traffic improvement (meaning the construction, extension and re-alignment of thoroughfares, particularly trunk routes) would benefit commerce immediately, particularly on the Slope. Shopkeepers and landowners of Smith Street, for example, expected that their property 'would be materially enhanced in value by the traffic from Heidelberg and the adjoining district passing through it, which traffic in the meantime was diverted to other districts' (e.g., Brunswick Street, Fitzroy).[2] Country traffic would benefit not only shopkeepers and publicans but also (important for plebeian Collingwood) artisans such as builders, wheelwrights and shoemakers.

However, East Collingwood was too impoverished to accomplish both kinds of improvement simultaneously and unaided. Therefore local political activity during the ensuing decades involved continual dilemmas: the priority of drainage or traffic improvement; the interests of the Slope versus those of the Flat; the advantages of the short term versus those of the long term; the welfare of particular groups (traders and, later, industrialists) versus the welfare of the whole community.

In December 1853 an East Collingwood Local Committee was formed, with a paid secretary, to seek road improvements and drainage. Being pessimistic about the benefits of annexation to the City of Melbourne, the Committee demanded an independent local government, with power to levy rates. The Committee also campaigned for a postal delivery service and for local police protection. Appropriately the Committee met at a newly established church called the Independent Chapel.

Despite the lapse of a century, it is still possible to assess the character of the Local Committee. The first step is to compile a list of the Committee's most prominent members. This is done by analysing reports of the Committee's activities in the Melbourne *Argus* in 1853–4 and by tracing letters and petitions from the committee to the Victorian government. These letters and petitions are preserved in the Chief Secretary's Records in the State Archives. From these sources, fifteen members appear to be particularly conspicuous. Next, we obtain the occupations and addresses of these men as shown in the 1856 parliamentary electoral roll and in petitions. If the fifteen are ranked in four groups (as in our analysis of census statistics in chapter 2), they are shown to be chiefly artisans and small businessmen:

A	B	C	D	Occupation unknown
2 merchants	1 storekeeper	1 clerk(?)	nil	1
1 gentleman	1 publican	1 compositor		
	1 grocer	3 carpenters		
		1 bootmaker		
		1 cabinetmaker		
		1 builder		
3	3	8	0	1

This confirms a comment by Geoffrey Serle in *The Golden Age* (1962) that, in movements for new municipalities in Victoria in the 1850s, the initiative generally came from small tradesmen. Furthermore, in East Collingwood, these tradesmen were concentrated in one part of the district. Of the fifteen men in our list, the addresses of fourteen can be traced and all these were on the Slope—including five in Wellington Street (then East Collingwood's busiest street), two in Smith Street and a couple in each of three other streets in between these two. The Flat, which accounted for most

38

of East Collingwood's territory and half of its population, was unrepresented.

The Local Committee's campaign came at an opportune time. During 1854 outlying parts of the municipality of Melbourne— today's municipalities of Port Melbourne, South Melbourne and Richmond—were demanding that Melbourne be divided into smaller municipalities. These moves were resisted by the Melbourne City Council but were favoured by the government. It was said that Victorian politicians did not want the Melbourne City Council to overshadow parliament. The government briefly considered creating a new northern municipality by severing Fitzroy Ward from the city and merging it with East Collingwood, but influential Fitzroy citizens objected to this uneven match. Finally, in 1855, East Collingwood was granted a municipality of its own. This move aroused no significant opposition. Indeed, the Central Road Board, the sole existing authority in East Collingwood, was glad to dispose of its expensive responsibilities there. The East Collingwood case became a precedent, and shortly afterwards South Melbourne, Port Melbourne and Richmond were also declared municipalities. This involved severing a considerable amount of territory from the City of Melbourne. Later, North Melbourne, Flemington and Fitzroy also severed from the city, although North Melbourne and Flemington eventually rejoined it. There was a severance move, too, in Carlton, but Melbourne City Council successfully resisted this.

The new municipal system led initially to boundary disputes. The East Collingwood Local Committee sought permission for East Collingwood to annex Clifton Hill, which was then mostly Crown land. This move was resisted by Melbourne City Council, which owned a quarry in Clifton Hill, and by Clifton Hill's dozen or so landowners (chiefly successful building contractors) who lived next to the quarry. One of these contractors, Henry Groom, was a city councillor. 'The freeholders of Clifton Hill', he said, 'have no desire to depreciate the value of their property by suffering it to be annexed to a swamp, which to drain itself would drain our resources.'[3] Clifton Hill's resistance campaign coincided with the newspaper sensation in 1855 over 'destitution in Collingwood' (see pp. 33–4). This helps to explain why leading East Collingwood citizens were eager to qualify the destitution reports as exaggerated.

The East Collingwood Local Committee wanted Clifton Hill for three purposes: to extend East Collingwood's north-south streets (Smith, Wellington and Hoddle Streets) northward to tap the traffic and trade coming from country areas such as Heidelberg; to gain access to the quarrying area for street-making materials; and for space for erecting public buildings. Without Clifton Hill, East Collingwood would have no Crown land. The government agreed to the East Collingwood request. The Clifton Hill quarrymen, although rebuffed, soon began profiting as stonework contractors to their new local council.

The government, however, refused to let East Collingwood annex Studley Park (across the Yarra). Today this remains part of the middle-class municipality of Kew.

Despite the success of the Local Committee, East Collingwood's trades people did not remain united. Unlike other Australian and English towns, East Collingwood lacked a civic and economic hub—a marketplace or civic square or even a single main street. The speculative ground-plan had dispersed business along several streets —Johnston, Victoria, Wellington and Smith Streets—and these streets now began to compete for traffic and trade and for increases in land values.

In 1855, a bad year economically, there was widespread interest among suburban businessmen and landowners in creating a trunk thoroughfare running from east to west through the northern half of the metropolis—a ring-road that would enable traffic to by-pass Melbourne proper. The road would connect the main northern suburbs: East Collingwood, Fitzroy, Carlton, Hotham (later renamed North Melbourne) and Flemington. To the west of Collingwood, the route would lead to the outer suburbs of Footscray and Williamstown, to the inland gold towns and even to Sydney. To the east, by means of a bridge over the Yarra, it would reach through rural Boroondara (Kew and Camberwell) to goldfields at Warrandyte on the Upper Yarra. Along this route, it was expected, land values and business would be increased. Also, the public works would provide employment for the building trades, which at this time lacked sufficient government and Melbourne City Council contracts.

Three alternative routes (which we shall call X, Y and Z) were proposed. Each was supported by owners of property, or of business, on the route concerned, and each was championed by a member of the Legislative Council—Victoria's parliament.

Route X: This route was based on Johnston Street, with a bridge over the Yarra at Johnston Street. In East Collingwood it was supported by interests in Portions 73 and 81 (on the Slope) and along Johnston Street. The leading spokesman for this group was John Pascoe Fawkner, M.L.C., who owned three houses in Smith Street (Portion 73). In Carlton this route was blocked by the grounds of the new University of Melbourne, and Route X interests campaigned (unsuccessfully) for a road through the university grounds in order to reach the Sydney and goldfield roads.

Route Y: This route was based on Queensberry Street (North Melbourne), Gertrude Street (Fitzroy) and Gipps Street (East Collingwood), with a bridge over the Yarra at Gipps Street. In East Collingwood this route was supported by interests in Portions 52–56, and along Gipps Street. The leading spokesman was Thomas Rae, who came from Scotland in 1847 and became a principal of Rae, Dickson and Company, merchants and soap and candle manufacturers. In 1855 the firm bought the Glasshouse, the most prominent landmark along Route Y on the Flat, for use as a candle factory. Rae entered the Legislative Council in 1855. Route Y, it was said, would bring country traffic to the centre of Collingwood; and the formation of Gipps Street would help to drain the Flat. However, Route Y was hampered by faulty street alignments in East Collingwood (in Portions 52–53) and by the Carlton Gardens (later the site of Melbourne's Exhibition Building). Its supporters briefly considered demolishing a few houses to connect Gipps Street with Fitzroy's Webb Street, but this became less practicable as more buildings rose. For the next twenty years Route Y interests campaigned (ultimately without success) for a road through the Carlton Gardens. In 1870 James McKean, who was both a Fitzroy councillor and a cabinet minister, was responsible for having the road proclaimed, but, following opposition from Melbourne City Council, the decision was later rescinded.

Route Z: This route was based on Victoria Parade, with a bridge over the Yarra at Church Street between Portions 59 and 60. It was supported by landowners along Victoria Street East, led by Francis Murphy, M.L.C., chairman of the Central Road Board, who lived at Mayfield in Portion 59. This route, they claimed, had the additional advantage of connecting with a possible trunk thoroughfare running from north to south along Church Street (Richmond), then over another bridge and along Chapel Street (Prahran) toward Brighton. However, opponents pointed out that Route Z would draw traffic merely to the fringes of Collingwood, not through it.

Thus began the battle of the Collingwood bridges. From the viewpoint of Kew, scope existed for one bridge, or perhaps two, but certainly not three. Because of the meandering of the Yarra, all three routes would lead on the Kew side into a single thoroughfare —Studley Park Road.

Route Z interests late in 1855 formed the Studley Park Bridge Company, and called for tenders. Spokesmen for Routes X and Y jointly protested. J. P. Fawkner said suspiciously:

> I found that on an out-of-the-way elbow of the Yarra, where few persons resided, a new road ending abruptly at the River Yarra, and close to the house and grounds of the president of the [Central] Road Board, had been made and macadamized without costing (as the president of the Road Board said) one shilling to the government . . . by the contractors for government roads . . . When, lo!, a new bridge company was started.[4]

The project, Fawkner said, was merely 'a job to increase the value of lands in that neighbourhood'.

While Route Z interests were beginning construction, supporters of Route X and Route Y competed for control of the remaining possible bridge. Their fight was the main feature of the first East Collingwood municipal council, elected in October 1855. Although the south (particularly Portions 52 and 53) was more densely populated than the north, the Route X faction gained control of the council and set the pace for the next five years. Each October, three of the seven councillors had to retire to seek re-election. A study of the council's minute books shows that, after each annual election, the alignment was as follows:[5]

	Oct. 1855	Oct. 1856	Oct. 1857	Oct. 1858	Oct. 1859
Faction X (north)	4	4	3	3	4
Faction Y (south)	2	2	3	3	3
Other	1	1	1	1	–

There were several reasons for this imbalance. First, until 1864 the municipality was not divided into wards; therefore, it would have been quite legal for candidates from the Route X area to gain the whole seven seats if they were able. Secondly, the Route Y area, being more populous, usually fielded more candidates (at least for the first two or three years) than the Route X area did; and, as there was no preferential system, the southern voters were spread thinly over this large field. This situation is shown statistically by analysing the first five elections (including both general and by-elections) until (and including) October 1858, as recorded in the council minute books:

	Total candidates	Elected	Not elected
Faction X	14	8	6
Faction Y	20	7	13
Other	2	2	0

Thirdly, the electoral procedure was open to abuse. Candidates were nominated at a rally, usually noisy, held on a vacant allotment on the Slope. On election day, voting (not by secret ballot) took place at several hotels, where voters could be treated with liquor. Allegations of malpractice were frequent. For example, in 1855, when John Pascoe Fawkner (patron of Faction X) was returning officer, he allegedly insulted persons who voted for Francis Murphy of Faction Z and was delighted finally to announce the victories of his own faction.

Accordingly, the first East Collingwood Council decided (on the motion of Faction X) that Collingwood's second bridge should be at Johnston Street, not Gipps Street. In this it had the support of Fitzroy interests who expected that Route X would bring more traffic and trade to Fitzroy than Route Y would. The council set about obtaining a government grant for the bridge, and began its unsuccessful campaign for the extension of Johnston Street westwards through the University grounds. Both bridges—Routes X and Z—were built in 1857, and were welcomed as a boost to the Collingwood economy. They provided work for local builders and carriers. And a subdivider near the Johnston Street bridge advertised that his allotments were now rendered 'the most valuable in Collingwood'. Meanwhile, Gipps Street, where Route Y would have crossed the Yarra, remained a swamp, and Faction Y plotted revenge.

After the battle of the bridges, the next crucial issue at stake in the geographical rivalry was the location of future municipal buildings—firstly council chambers and secondly a possible market. It was universally assumed that these buildings would become the hub of the district and would bring increased traffic, trade and land values to their immediate surroundings. For the council chambers (including a court-house and police lock-up), Faction X forced the council to buy a site in Johnston Street (in Portion 73 on the Slope). Faction Y unsuccessfully protested that priority ought to be given to more essential works 'bearing on the comfort and health of the inhabitants'. The municipality's 'centre of gravity' remained in Johnston Street on the Slope for the next thirty years. (In the

1880s, after the Flat had become habitable and commercially useful, the centre swung towards the south and the Flat, with the construction of a boom-style town hall on a reclaimed swamp in Portion 66, Hoddle Street.)

Factional feeling rose even more over the question of a marketplace. Faction Y advocated somewhere south of Gipps Street (meaning Portions 52 to 55). A public meeting in favour of this view was chaired by Thomas Rae (the patron of Faction Y), whose Glasshouse candleworks happened to be in that area. Faction X insisted on Portion 74 (adjoining Johnston Street), through which the central drain (see p. 35) then ran. The council's official survey plan of 1856 shows 'proposed sites for markets, baths, wash houses, etc.', superimposed over the drain. However, the council's negotiations with the owner of Portion 74 failed. The council then decided to use some Crown land in Clifton Hill (at the intersection of Reilly Street and Heidelberg Road). Thus the municipal centre of gravity would have been moved even further north. However, the market was never built, and the Clifton Hill site was eventually sold to raise funds for municipal works. The marketplace issue of 1856 had implications for relations not only between north and south but also between the Slope and the Flat. It is significant that the council was giving priority to the planning of a market (i.e., facilities for commerce) rather than the planning of drainage or street construction (i.e., facilities for living). This priority appeared to be in the interests of the traders on the Slope rather than the families on the Flat.

The council also split over the construction of road surfaces. Faction Y unsuccessfully tried to give priority to the main business streets (which meant Portions 52 and 53 in the south). Faction X gave priority to making Hoddle Street north of Johnston Street so as to connect with the Clifton Hill quarries and with the northern country districts, 'thereby benefiting the whole municipality'. Moreover, Faction Y advocated (and Faction X resisted) expenditure on sanitary services (e.g., sweeping of streets and drains) which were particularly necessary in the more densely populated Faction Y area.

Exasperated, Faction Y proposed dividing the municipality into wards and increasing the number of councillors, thus reducing Faction X to about a quarter of the council. Faction X, naturally, outvoted this move. Faction Y argued that, on a population basis, the north was over-represented and that, as soon as one Faction X councillor raised his hand, his three colleagues always voted likewise. Furthermore, Faction X frequently shelved Faction Y's motions by referring them to the council's public works committee —and this committee was dominated by Faction X. Faction X replied that, in terms of area, the north (beyond Johnston Street) comprised more than half the municipality, even though much of the north (in Clifton Hill) was still vacant Crown land. A public meeting, called to hear ratepayers' views on wards, was evenly divided. The chairman, Thomas Rae, gave the decision in favour of wards, and the meeting ended in uproar. (Rae is an interesting figure. His influence was not confined to East Collingwood. He lived in Fitzroy, and was instrumental in severing Fitzroy from the City of Melbourne in 1858.)

During the regime of Faction X, the council regularly received petitions and protests from the Flat about the worsening drainage problem. The deterioration of the Flat, said its residents, resulted from 'artificial, not natural causes'. Water from the higher areas was being conveyed to the Flat with increased efficiency; as well as sewage, it included garbage and even the carcasses of animals; it dislodged frail wooden bridges that had been built here and there across the central drain; it cut off the ends of streets, requiring residents to make inconvenient detours to reach shopping centres; it flooded the interiors of houses. The problem was worst along Gipps Street (in the heart of Faction Y's area), where the central drain ran into a creek and gully on its slow journey to the Yarra. The Faction X regime, however, resolved that priority in drainage works would be given to the north-west of the municipality, with particular attention to Portions 81 and 80. Firstly the council constructed a drain through Portion 86, resulting in storm-water being expedited southwards along the central drain towards Faction Y's area. Then, more significantly, it resolved to co-operate with Melbourne City Council in cutting a major open drain along Reilly Street (afterwards re-named Alexandra Parade) from Smith Street to the Yarra.

Faction X expected that the Reilly Street drain would drain the Crown lands of Clifton Hill, enabling them to be sold and populated, and incidentally increasing traffic, trade and land values in Faction X's area. Faction Y pleaded that a major drain be constructed further south through 'the Flat proper' near Gipps Street, but Faction X ruled that the Reilly Street drain would be sufficient to make the Flat 'tenantable'. However, as soon as it was constructed, the Reilly Street drain proved to be a failure. In winter the drain overflowed southward on to the Flat. Then Melbourne

City Council and the new Fitzroy Council began extending the drain through Fitzroy to Carlton, bringing even more water down to East Collingwood and necessitating an expensive enlargement of the East Collingwood section. The completed drain, about 10 ft deep, was lined with stone; it was partly fenced in, and crossed by wooden bridges. Occasionally someone fell in and was drowned.

Alienated from the council, residents along Route Y (especially Portions 56, 57, 58) formed a militant pressure group outside the council—the 'Local Committee of Collingwood Flat'. The Committee convened protest meetings on the Flat and became the council's most persistent correspondent, submitting a petition, complaint or inquiry to almost every council meeting during several successive winters. Supported by Faction Y councillors, the Committee demanded that no more funds be spent on the Slope until a comparable share was spent on the Flat. At first, the working men of the Flat were discouraged from attending council meetings as observers or as councillors because Faction X insisted on daytime meetings, starting at 10 a.m. In 1857 Faction Y, conscious of its popular following, managed to institute evening meetings, which became so popular that a policeman was sometimes needed to maintain order.

Unfortunately for the historian, the Local Committee of the Flat is one of many significant groupings in Collingwood that have left no written records. Minutes of the Flat-dwellers' meetings, if we had them, would be as valuable as the minutes of the council. And if only we had a record of the unofficial proceedings in the public gallery of the council chambers . . .

One interesting question about the factionalism of 1855–60 is the role apparently played by Freemasonry. Collingwood was among the first districts in which Freemasonry became established outside Melbourne. As one would expect, the organization's influence is now difficult to document, although it was probably well known in the face-to-face community of Collingwood at that time. The following significant remark about the first Collingwood council appears in a reminiscent article published in the Collingwood *Observer* in 1885, a generation later: 'Freemasonry seems to have exerted no little influence in the election of councillors as well as in the appointment of officers, for Mr J. J. Moody, then a prominent Freemason, was the first town clerk.'[6]

The article, written by *Observer* editor J. M. Tait in collaboration with Moody himself, does not elaborate this point. However, from other sources (e.g., council minutes, newspaper reports, and records at the Victorian Freemasons' headquarters) it is possible to reconstruct the following account.

Moody was one of Victoria's most senior Masons. In 1854, for example, he was general director of ceremonies for the laying of the foundation stone of the Melbourne Gasworks with full Masonic honours. In Collingwood Moody was identified with Faction X. During his five years as town clerk, the factions continually clashed over the amount of his salary, Faction X favouring £300 and Faction Y favouring only about £200. (Faction Y's reasons were that sufficient applicants were prepared to accept the lower figure and that the council's funds were needed for public works.) When the Johnston Street bridge was instigated by Faction X in 1855, the cabinet minister responsible for such matters (Andrew Clarke, Surveyor-General) was a prominent Mason. When a supporter of Faction Y asked Clarke in 1855 for government funds for a Gipps Street bridge, Clarke refused. Yet the Johnston Street bridge did receive a government grant. The council's official half-yearly report (written by Moody) said that the Johnston Street bridge foundation stone was laid by 'the Hon. Capt. Andrew Clarke, M.L.A., Provincial Grand Master of Freemasons for Victoria, under the Grand Lodge of England, assisted by a numerous assemblage of the brethren, under the English, Irish and Scottish Grand Lodges'. There can be no doubt, then, that Faction X had strong Masonic connections through Moody and possibly also through a local Masonic lodge situated in Faction X's area. It would be helpful to obtain comparative data about the role of Freemasonry in local politics elsewhere in Victoria about this time.

Faction Y, too, might have had Masonic connections, but not to the same extent as Faction X and presumably not through the same local lodge. A Masonic lodge was established at a hotel in southern Smith Street—in Faction Y's area—early in 1857, a year or so after the establishment of the council and after the battle of the bridges. Two prominent members of that lodge were supporters of Faction Y; and one Faction Y councillor seems to have been a member there. If there were Masons in Faction Y, they were far less influential than in Faction X and represented a rival locality. Factional struggles within Freemasonry were not unknown.

The dominant influence in Faction Y evidently came from non-Masons. Oddfellows' lodges, for example, were active in East Collingwood politics. Between 1853 and 1858 four were established there. These were prominent in radical movements such as the eight-hours agitation. At least two of these lodges, possibly more, were located on the Flat, and they would presumably have been opposed to the Faction X regime.

The conflict between Factions X and Y reached a climax in 1859–60 when several issues erupted. First, a dispute occurred over a council election. A Faction X candidate, Benjamin Jarvis, was elected by a margin of one vote—the casting vote of the returning officer, who was a Faction X councillor. Secondly, Faction Y denounced town clerk Moody, alleging that he was in league with Faction X, that he exercised an undue influence over the council, and that he had mismanaged accounts. A public meeting of ratepayers demanded Moody's dismissal and the disbanding of the council. Faction Y resigned, but Faction X refused. Thirdly, Faction Y charged Faction X (who comprised the council's public works committee) with jobbery and corruption. The council's minute books provide some prima facie evidence for this allegation. E.g., Benjamin Jarvis of Faction X was elected to council on the nomination of one Henry Carter; two months later Carter was awarded a municipal building contract on the motion of Jarvis and another Faction X councillor. Consequently, in October 1860 the Faction X councillors retired in disgrace, and the largely new council dismissed Moody. The stage was now set for a new round of factionalism, involving new groupings and new issues.

Among the major pressure groups in municipal politics were the contractors who competed to supply materials or labour for road works. A contractor might become a councillor, or, more usually, might have friends on the council. These relationships formed complex chains, of which the following (reconstructed from council minutes and other sources) is a brief example. Samuel Ramsden, of the Clifton Hill quarries, was a councillor in 1857–9, and was particularly conspicuous when stonework was under discussion. Henry Groom, also of the Clifton Hill quarries, was a big supplier of stone to the council; he unsuccessfully sought election to the council in 1860, was a Fitzroy councillor in 1858–62, and later secured a position as Fitzroy borough overseer. Thomas Greenwood, a Collingwood councillor in 1856–65, was associated with Groom (and with another contractor, Thomas Grimwood) in a big Fitzroy kerbing contract. Grimwood, who contracted for Collingwood Council as well as for Fitzroy, nominated both Greenwood and Samuel Ramsden for Collingwood Council. Grimwood himself also stood for Collingwood Council, unsuccessfully. Green-

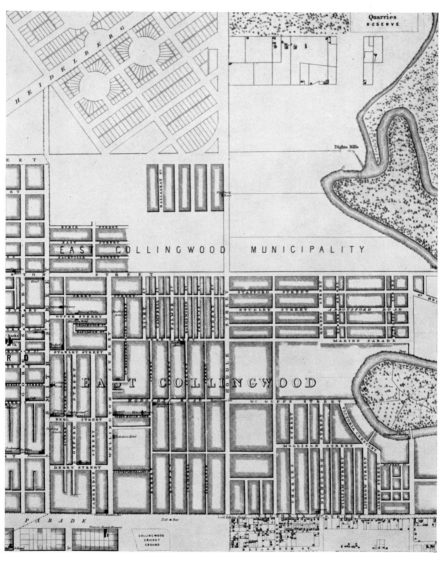

Collingwood in 1855, then called 'East' Collingwood.

View of Melbourne from the vicinity of the Eastern Hill (Fitzroy), 1846.

Brunswick Street, Fitzroy; watercolour by Mrs Richard Hanmer Dunbury, 1841, 'from the front of our house [looking] away from Melbourne'.

wood was also said to be allied with another influential contractor, Andrew Martin. In 1863, Greenwood became mayor, and simultaneously Martin was awarded the paid position of inspector of nuisances. Another contractor, Timothy Mahony, competed with Martin for favours, and was allied with yet another councillor. And so on . . .

A contractor or councillor was especially influential if he operated a hotel or was allied with a publican. Of the six men named in the previous paragraph, five owned or operated a hotel at some time in the 1850s or 1860s. A contractor with a hotel could provide a council candidate with headquarters and supporters. A councillor with a hotel could attract customers. In 1862 when Councillor Peter Petherick, of the Studley Arms Hotel, was chairman of the council's public works committee, an anonymous letter in the Collingwood *Observer* remarked: 'Being chairman of the public works committee, what more natural than that contractors and their men should flock to the bar of the Studley Arms where the landlord can dispense nobblers and patronage at the same time.' Another letter (signed by a ratepayer) said: 'Why, it is a fortune to any enterprising being to get elected municipal councillor.'[7]

Contacts between councillors and contractors were facilitated by lodges, which met at hotels. Lodges provided candidates for municipal and parliamentary elections. The aforementioned trio of Groom, Grimwood and Greenwood were connected through the Oddfellows. Groom and Grimwood were members of Collingwood's first Oddfellows' lodge, founded in 1853, and in 1858 these two men were prominent in founding the third Oddfellows' lodge, which met at Councillor Greenwood's Yorkshire Stingo Hotel (in Hoddle Street, on the Flat). In 1861 Greenwood unsuccessfully contested the Collingwood seat in the Legislative Assembly, coming last in a field of eight. A fourth Oddfellows' lodge—also founded in 1858 on the Flat—met at Charles Swift's Willow Tree Hotel (Portion 67). Two officials of this lodge—Swift himself and George David Langridge—both entered the council in 1865, and Langridge entered parliament in 1874. Campaign manager for Swift and Langridge was Richard Cooke, a builder and political activist who settled on the Flat about 1860. Cooke became prominent in the Ancient Order of Foresters, another popular Collingwood society. Clearly the political role of local lodges, which can be indicated only briefly here, is worth further investigation.

Councillors enjoyed many perquisites. The three members of the public works committee commonly used council labour and mater-

E

ials to improve the streets and lanes where they or fellow councillors lived or had businesses, or where they hoped to win votes at election time. Peter Petherick, who was rate collector from 1856 to 1860 and a councillor from 1860 to 1864, consistently neglected to pay rates on his own property during both periods.[8] And then there was a baker who joined the council because he believed (wrongly) that councillors were paid; incompetent, he was persuaded by his constituents to resign.

The Collingwood climate of the 1850s is hard to document fully. Although a weekly newspaper (the *Observer*) began serving East Collingwood and Fitzroy in 1857, it consisted largely of official proceedings—councils, courts and public meetings. The really significant news circulated orally in hotels, in streets, at water standpipes, in lodges, in working men's clubs and unions and at ratepayers' meetings. And for decades a familiar figure was the 'bellman' or town crier, who operated under licence from the council on behalf of private clients. It was a village-like community, with emphasis on face-to-face relationships. This being before the advent of the large employing organization, work was not as separated from other everyday activities as it was later to become. True, a clerk or printing compositor would travel daily to the central workplace of his employers, but, judging from the description of occupants of dwellings in the ratebook, the typical Collingwood man (if there was one) worked either at his home address (as a shopkeeper, publican, bootmaker or smith), or at the address of a neighbour (as an apprentice or assistant), or at no fixed address (as a building contractor, carpenter, builder's labourer, cabman or street-sweeper), and he was probably self-employed (or at least an 'assistant' to a self-employed man) rather than an anonymous employee in a bureaucratic organization. Despite its booming population of 10,786 in 1857 and 12,653 in 1861, East Collingwood still retained a rural appearance. The council offered a bounty of 2s 6d a head on dead snakes. Butchers from Melbourne and Collingwood held grazing leases on the Clifton Hill Crown lands and on the Flat's vacant paddocks. Collingwood's small dairymen, objecting to the monopolistic butchers, sought (unsuccessfully) to have Clifton Hill declared a free common for the cow-keeping public.

These first years of the East Collingwood Council saw the gradual introduction of a few civic amenities, though for the benefit of the Slope rather than the Flat.

In 1856 the Sewerage and Water Commission extended Melbourne's new reticulated water supply to East Collingwood, in the form of a pipe leading from a tank on the eastern hill to a solitary fountain (called a 'standpipe') in Smith Street, Portion 68. By 1858 the commission had installed several other fountains as far east as Hoddle Street, as well as a hundred fire hydrants. To save money, the council would have preferred fewer hydrants, spaced farther apart, but the commission graciously accepted payment in instalments. After 1858 water was connected directly to private premises along the main roads but many side streets on the Flat were still without piped water in 1870.

However, in East Collingwood, piped water was as much a curse as a blessing, for the government neglected to implement a metropolitan sewerage scheme. Compared with water supply, sewerage seemed more difficult (it needed a network of individual household connections from the outset, not merely a few public standpipes). It also seemed less productive and less profitable. All household and industrial drainage entered the open street-channels, all gravitating towards the Yarra. This was no worry for comfortable people living high and dry on the Hill in Fitzroy (or in comparable areas in East Melbourne, western Richmond or south of the Yarra), or even on the East Collingwood Slope, but it was disastrous for the Flat. For example, water used for washing beer barrels at a brewery in Portion 73 on the Slope flowed down to Portion 74 on the Flat, where it stagnated in the central drain. The brewer claimed that carting the liquid away was too expensive and the Sewerage and Water Commission was reluctant to allow precious water to be 'wasted' on flushing public drains from fire hydrants. Similar nuisances arose from butchers' shops, where blood and offal were flushed into the streets, and from hotels, where running water was used to create a water closet.

The early council directed much energy towards improving communication in the streets. In the early 1850s when East Collingwood was the responsibility of the Central Road Board, toll gates operated in the few made roads such as Johnston Street and Victoria Street. As subdivisions developed, it became possible for traffic to avoid these gates by making short detours. In 1856, after the formation of the council with power of property taxation, the street tolls became unnecessary and were abolished. Tolls (and toll dodging) continued until the 1870s on the bridges connecting Collingwood with Kew, Heidelberg and Northcote. The abolition of bridge tolls facilitated Melbourne's sprawl to the other side of the Yarra during the land boom of the 1880s.

In 1857 the council managed to have East Collingwood's postal staff increased so as to extend the mail delivery service right across the Flat to the Yarra. The council also erected name-plates. (Previously visitors easily became lost in the street maze, and sometimes even residents did not know their own address but described their houses as being 'off' the nearest main thoroughfare.) In 1866 the council erected more street name-plates, and tried to persuade householders to affix house numbers. In the case of defaulters, the council affixed the number and requested payment (usually without success).

In the late 'fifties and early 'sixties the council scraped the carriageways of most streets and, more tardily, sprinkled loose metal on some of them. Favoured streets, especially on the Slope, were given gravel footpaths, with kerbs and channels of bluestone slabs (or sometimes kerbs of hardwood planks). Thus sewage and garbage could now be flushed, indeed swept, more efficiently on to the muddy Flat. The council was eager to speed up kerbing and metalling, for, as one councillor said, this would 'greatly increase the value of all property, occasion a much larger annual amount of municipal rates being collected from the new houses, shops and other buildings erected in consequence of such improvements, and promote the trade of the district by such increase of population'. However, the council lacked finance. It sought unsuccessfully to raise a loan of £10,000. The government was giving a subsidy of two to one on local rates, but the council, consisting of property owners, stubbornly kept rates down and lost much government assistance. Later in the century, rates doubled while the government subsidy dwindled away.

At the insistence of business ratepayers, council workmen gave the main business streets a daily spraying with water to keep down dust. In 1865 Smith Street business people demanded three daily waterings there, and in 1877 draper Mark Foy demanded a fourth. Other streets were less fortunate. Hoddle Street in 1866 was being watered only as far as the house of a certain councillor, although when this fact became publicized the rest of Hoddle Street received some water too. However, the residential streets on the Flat were ignored and remained dusty in summer, muddy in winter.

In 1856 the Melbourne Gas Company's mains reached the Slope, lighting the shops but, while the streets of Melbourne (and later Fitzroy) became gaslit, the poorer East Collingwood Council continued to rely on publicans' kerosene lamps (required by law outside hotels). In 1857 the council bought twenty-three old kerosene lamps, discarded by the Melbourne City Council. A Collingwood Gas Company was established in 1860 (with works in Reilly Street, North Fitzroy, and a duplicate network of street mains), but the two companies allegedly co-operated in keeping street-lighting charges up; both quoted about £13 per gas lamp per annum (compared with only £9 10s per lamp quoted by kerosene-lighting contractors). In 1862 Fitzroy Council, to spite the gas companies, reverted temporarily to the inferior kerosene, and managed to have the gas price per lamp reduced to £10 in 1864 and £7 in 1866. By 1865, when publicans' lamps were no longer compulsory, East Collingwood's streets were dismal indeed, with only 83 municipal lamps compared with 145 in Fitzroy, an interesting contrast. In 1864 East Collingwood began converting its lamps to gas, although even in the late 1870s some still used kerosene. When several side streets each asked for a lamp, one councillor grumbled that at this rate every street in East Collingwood would want one and he 'would like to know where the money was to come from to pay for them'.

One of the earliest questions considered by the council was the possibility of public baths. In the 1850s and 1860s private bath-rooms (and even bathtubs) were a rarity. To bathe, a Collingwood resident had to either use primitive methods (a bucket or dish in the bedroom, kitchen or back-yard), or swim in the Yarra (usually prohibited by the council as a nuisance, with a £5 fine), or travel a discouraging distance to the city baths or to bayside sea-baths. As mentioned earlier, baths and laundries were included in the council's unsuccessful plans for a public marketplace in Portion 74 in 1856. In 1857 the government offered to let municipalities build baths on Crown land, but the council regarded East Colling-wood's Crown land in Clifton Hill as too remote from the population for bathing purposes. (This incident highlights a constant problem of East Collingwood and Fitzroy; the settlement developed on private land, while the nearest Crown land, needed for civic amenities, was situated inconveniently outside the settlement.) In 1865, when Victoria feared a cholera outbreak, interest in baths revived briefly: some Fitzroy shopkeepers (e.g., a hair-dresser) offered hot or cold baths to the public, and Fitzroy Council briefly considered converting part of its future town hall site into a public bath-house. To some councillors, a bath-house, being self-supporting, seemed more attractive than other public works. The *Observer* commented that bathing facilities would not only benefit the public health but would also make the lower classes clean enough to attend church 'instead of spending Sunday in tiresome idleness'. However, for the rest of the nineteenth century both suburbs remained without municipal baths.

Meanwhile, although bathrooms became common in houses built after about 1880 (e.g., in Clifton Hill), they remained lacking in many houses in older Collingwood. In 1914 a Royal Commission on housing in Melbourne was told that one Collingwood street had twenty houses but only three baths.[9] In 1937 Victoria's Housing Investigation and Slum Abolition Board declared that the absence of baths in houses was one of the criteria of a slum.

THE SUBURB WITH BAD BREATH

(Collingwood, 1860–70, compared with Fitzroy)

4

One factor affecting a suburb's social standing was its state of health as measured by mortality statistics. During the nineteenth century, Australia was continually threatened by 'zymotic' (i.e., acute infectious) diseases—diarrhoea, dysentery, typhus-like fevers, scarlet fever, diphtheria, measles and smallpox. In Victoria in 1854–62 these diseases caused between a quarter and a half of all deaths each year.

Before the impact of bacteriology in the 1880s, the most influential conception of disease in Australia, as elsewhere, was the 'miasmatic' one. According to this, disease was caused not by microscopic living organisms passing from one person to another (as in the later germ theory) but by bad air (as in 'mal-aria'). Even when the disease was recognized as being communicable from person to person (e.g., plague, leprosy and smallpox), the 'contagion' was conceived as chemical (a vapour or miasma emanating from the patient or from his wounds), not as biological. In most diseases common in Victoria, person-to-person contact was less obvious; here the ruling assumption was that the bad air emanated from filth in the environment—from swamps, stagnant pools, dirty rivers and accumulations of decomposing manure and garbage.

In Victoria the leading exponent of miasma theory was the Central Board of Health, which had been set up by the government in 1855 to advise the government and the municipalities on public health. The Board comprised a full-time chairman (Dr William McCrae) and about half a dozen part-time members, usually including several medical practitioners and perhaps a police magistrate and a parliamentarian. In its reports to parliament and local councils, the Board regularly attributed the spread of disease to 'atmospheric causes, such as the prevalence of easterly winds, sudden and unusual changes of temperature, and impurities produced by the exhalations from stagnant water'.

As the miasma theory implied that a damp or smelly place was an unhealthy place, it had unfortunate implications for East Collingwood—the dampest and smelliest suburb of Melbourne. There seemed to be a high correlation between East Collingwood's miasma and its mortality statistics. In 1858, a comparatively 'good' year for the rest of Victoria, Collingwood's mortality rose alarmingly—from 24 deaths per 1,000 persons to 32. In 1861, when mortality rose throughout Victoria because of epidemics of measles and scarlet fever, East Collingwood still stood out, as shown in these government statistics (deaths per 1,000 inhabitants) for the metropolitan area:[1]

East Collingwood	28
South Melbourne and Port Melbourne	26
Fitzroy	24
Melbourne proper	23 (est.)
South Yarra and Prahran	23
Richmond	21
North Melbourne and Carlton	20
St Kilda and Brighton	17

East Collingwood was noted for its child mortality: of all deaths in East Collingwood in 1861, 71 per cent were under five years, compared with only 62 per cent in Fitzroy and 57 per cent in the whole metropolis; out of all inhabitants aged under five in East Collingwood in 1861, 10 per cent died, compared with only 9 per cent in Fitzroy and 8 per cent in the whole metropolis.

It is wise to be cautious now in discussing such nineteenth-century mortality statistics for they are not as exact and as illuminating as they once seemed. Firstly, local registrars in Victoria did not confine their registrations to deaths occurring within their own districts. Were the widows and deserted wives of East Collingwood less likely than Fitzroy fathers to travel to the city to register their children's deaths? Secondly, the death rate of 23 per 1,000 given above for Melbourne proper (today's central business district) excludes estimated deaths of suburban persons at the Melbourne Hospital; if the excluded deaths were allocated to the suburbs, the suburban figures would be higher than shown. But which suburbs? To what extent were the plebeian sick of Collingwood less likely to receive hospital treatment than the patrician sick of St Kilda and Brighton?

However, the Central Board of Health interpreted the statistics to suit its miasma doctrine. East Collingwood's alarming mortality, it said in 1859, was caused by the district's moist soil and contaminated air: 'The evaporation of the surplus moisture lowers temperatures, produces chills, and creates or aggravates the sudden changes or fluctuations of temperature by which health is injured.' The Central Board of Health criticized the extension of dwellings ('more especially of the poorer classes') on the Flat. It noted that the central drain on the Flat was accumulating 'every kind of filth, the emanations from which contaminated the air in every direction'. The C.B.H. recommended that the central drain be replaced by an underground pipe, but the council in 1861 lined the drain with bluestone and left it open.

In 1861 the C.B.H. was suprised to learn that, although the Flat and the Slope had equal populations, the number of deaths in 1860 was much greater on the Slope. The C.B.H. wondered (probably correctly, according to twentieth-century theory) whether this had something to do with the Slope's greater density of population, and commented: 'It appears that Collingwood Flat does not deserve the unenviable distinction which it has obtained of being the most unhealthy spot around Melbourne.'

Medical practitioners in East Collingwood and Fitzroy, as elsewhere, sometimes thought in terms of miasma theory, although not as much as the Central Board of Health did. In its report of 1859, the C.B.H. triumphantly attributed miasmatist statements to two prominent local doctors. Dr A. C. Livingstone, of East Collingwood, was quoted as blaming imperfect drainage for much of the local mortality from diphtheria, scarlet fever and measles: 'No class of diseases is more clearly traceable to bad drainage than the malignant affections of the throat'. Dr R. T. Tracy, of Fitzroy, was quoted as saying that a diphtheria outbreak in North Fitzroy probably arose from large disused brick-holes, now containing stagnant water and used as rubbish dumps. Similarly, the local press reported that another Fitzroy doctor, after attending a sick family for five months without much success, blamed 'an accumulation of stagnant water near their residence'.

In making such diagnoses, these practitioners were doing the best they could within the limitations of the medical knowledge of their time. Not knowing about micro-organisms and not fully understanding the functioning of the human organism, they naturally related their diagnoses to a macro-organism—the town. They therefore prescribed public works. However, unlike the Central Board, the local medical practitioners often diverged from orthodox miasma theory. For example, referring to East Collingwood's high infant mortality, Dr Livingstone said in 1863:

That some of this mortality is due to our defective sanitary condition does not admit of a doubt; but the principal cause is the increased heat [during summer], and it is desirable that every precaution should be taken to guard against its effects. The best safeguard is the cold bath daily administered to the child. I am afraid that this expedient is much neglected by all classes, for which there is no excuse, as water is now abundant.[2]

And a non-miasmatist view was taken by the Collingwood *Observer* in 1865—that East Collingwood's high mortality rate was caused not by geography but by the fact that 'the miserable low-rented huts attract a class of residents among whom, no doubt, there is much disease, arising from poverty or improvidence'.

Nevertheless, the miasmatist concept of disease remained pervasive, being supported, as it was, by the daily evidence of eyes and nose. As the local press put it, 'numerous foul and dangerous nuisances have made the Flat most unsavoury in the nostrils of the public and a name of reproach far beyond the boundaries of the borough'. A local churchman commented in 1866 that, because of this combination of unhealthiness and poverty,

> East Collingwood . . . has . . . obtained an unenviable notoriety, and is despised and avoided as a place of residence by many of those living in higher, aristocratic and more favoured localities, and much odium is often attempted to be cast upon it and its inhabitants.[3]

East Collingwood's drainage and 'miasma' became a lively issue early in 1861, after heavy rains (and flooding from Fitzroy) had come on top of several epidemics. The influence of miasmatic theory can be seen in several items appearing in the press within a few days.[4] First, a jury at an inquest declared that one East Collingwood patient had died from congestion of the lungs, caused by the district's 'inefficient drainage'. Secondly, an editorial in the Melbourne *Argus* said that diphtheria and other malignant diseases of the throat in East Collingwood were being caused by 'the deadly marsh vapours which enveloped this pestiferous swamp after the recent flood'. Criticizing East Collingwood Council for its inactivity on sanitation, the *Argus* added:

> Almost every street lying upon the Flat has its green and stagnant gutter, or its foetid pool, while the backyards of many of the dairymen, car-proprietors, and others, unprovided with any kind of drainage, teem with decomposed matter, the effluvia of which are quite as pungent and quite as varied as those . . . in Cologne and Cairo. After a

heavy rain . . . Collingwood Flat is scarcely less insalubrious than the Pontine Marshes at the height of summer.

Thirdly, a letter in the *Argus* said that the Flat 'is rapidly becoming one cesspool, the exhalations from which are every year becoming worse'.

East Collingwood Council decided to grasp this opportunity to seek a drainage system for the district. The council asked the government for an East Collingwood Improvement Bill, empowering the council to compulsorily acquire land for drainage purposes. However, the Bill drafted by the business-oriented council was for traffic improvements rather than drainage. It provided chiefly for the widening and extending of streets. Drainage was to result only incidentally, by the level of east-west streets being lowered to facilitate gravitation.

But which streets were to be favoured? Early in 1861, after the northern faction in the council (Faction X, in chapter 3) had been defeated, the council became dominated by new councillors representing southern interests. The new councillors (whom we shall call Faction Q) wished to give priority to creating a new southern thoroughfare. This was to be an extension of Fitzroy's Gertrude Street (along a line that was later named Langridge Street) to connect with the Studley Park bridge leading to Kew. The increase in traffic and trade was expected to improve southern land values.

Who were these councillors and what were their interests? We can find out by doing a great deal of 'detective work' on numerous sources: council minute books, newspapers, parliamentary electoral rolls, street directories, Titles Office property-ownership records, council ratebooks and Clement Hodgkinson's survey plans. This research reveals that, in mid-1861, Faction Q comprised six of the seven councillors. Of these, four had property interests along the proposed route. First (reading from west to east) there was Councillor Henry Turnbull, who owned property in Portion 53 at the north-east corner of Wellington and Elizabeth Streets (a bootmaker's shop in the former and a wooden house in the latter.) Elizabeth Street, then a muddy alley, was to be widened as part of Route Q, making this corner suddenly one of the most valuable in Collingwood. Secondly, Route Q went along the side fence of the Yorkshire Stingo Hotel, Hoddle Street (Portion 56), owned by Councillor Thomas Greenwood. Thirdly, Route Q crossed Henry Street (Portion 56), in which Councillor John Noone, a lithographer in the Lands Department, had a house. (About this time,

Noone also bought a house in Hoddle Street, not far from Greenwood's hotel.) Fourthly, the route crossed Charles Street (Portion 57), where Councillor John Newlands, a shipping agent and valuer, had houses and land.

Faction Q's fifth and sixth members—George Payne and James Houghton—were close political associates of Turnbull. Payne, a house-painting contractor, owned fifteen houses and four shops, chiefly in Portions 52 and 53 not far from (but not exactly on) Route Q. Houghton was a grocer, several blocks from Route Q; according to the *Observer*, he admitted that the improvement Bill would benefit the streets and properties of his friends.

The East Collingwood Improvement Bill was introduced in the Legislative Assembly early in 1862 by Charles Jardine Don, M.L.A., who (as will be explained fully in chapter 6) was an associate of Faction Q. The Route Q plan alarmed the rest of East Collingwood. Graham Berry, M.L.A. (one of the other two Collingwood members, who was a rival of Charles Don), took up the cause of the objectors. Berry, who then owned the Collingwood *Observer* (1861–4), wrote editorials denouncing the 'selfishness and folly' of the Bill. Route Q, being based on no topographical survey, was irrelevant to drainage, he said. The route was chosen only to form a continuation of a business street in Fitzroy. The plan, Berry said, would bankrupt the municipality in order to increase the value of one part—the promoters' part.

Inside the council, the Route Q plan was immediately opposed by publican Peter Petherick, who represented the north (Portion 73) and who for a while was the only councillor not a member of Faction Q. Later, the plan was also opposed by three new councillors. They were industrialists who were primarily interested in making the Flat useful for industry. The Flat, they said, needed drainage rather than merely new streets, and this could be achieved by using underground pipes. (At this time, underground drains were a novelty in Australia.)

Early in 1863 Faction Q and its opponents reached a compromise. They agreed to a modified, less expensive version of Route Q. At the eastern end, Route Q was to stop far short of Studley Park bridge; at the western end, it was to stop at Wellington Street. (The connection with Gertrude Street, Fitzroy, was not completed until the 1880s.)

Meanwhile, voters in other parts of the municipality had taken alarm. By 1864 Faction Q had lost its majority in the council. The new council delayed beginning any improvement works until 1867.

In 1864 a property-owner in the line of Route Q became impatient and tried to get elected to the council with Route Q as his main policy. He was Joseph Berry, an ironmonger, who owned the south-east corner of Wellington and Elizabeth Streets (a wooden shop in the former and two wooden cottages in the latter). Under the Route Q plan, the council was to buy Berry's frontages at good prices to widen Elizabeth Street. At the election, Joseph Berry came last out of six candidates. A few months later, under new Victorian legislation regulating local government, East Collingwood became divided into wards (three wards, each with three councillors), and it was no longer possible for one corner to dominate the whole.

One reason for the delay in implementing improvement works was the council's lack of funds. In 1861, during the newspaper sensation about the danger of miasma and disease in East Collingwood, the council took the opportunity of asking the government for a special grant for East Collingwood improvement. In the age of *laissez-faire*, such government intervention was not normal. The council pleaded that a grant would help Victoria as well as Collingwood—it might prevent East Collingwood disease from spreading to other communities. And, as the government was helping to increase Victoria's population by a programme of migration from Britain, the government ought to help preserve Victoria's existing population (e.g., in East Collingwood). Richard Heales, who was leader of the Victorian government in 1861 and who had relatives and strong support in Collingwood, favoured granting £21,000 to East Collingwood, but his recommendation was opposed by other ministers, and anyway Heales left office before his recommendation could be implemented.

The council could, of course, obtain finance by increasing the local taxation on property, but there were several obstacles to this.

Firstly, East Collingwood's properties were less valuable than those elsewhere. In 1866 the government made a survey of rates and property values in all Victorian municipalities, and if we analyse the returns (in the State Archives) we find significant differences between East Collingwood and Fitzroy:

Net annual value	E. C'wood properties (%)	Fitzroy properties (%)
£100 and above	1	6
£50 — £99	3	14
£25 — £49	9	23
Under £25	87	57

(Net annual value means the annual rent which the site and all improvements upon it might reasonably be expected to return, less a deduction to cover rates.)

Secondly, an extraordinarily high proportion of East Collingwood's properties were vacant allotments, whose owners were unknown. The rate collector could not step in until building materials appeared on the site. By 1870 rate arrears amounting to £2,000 were owing on a thousand such allotments. Fitzroy, on the other hand, was one of the most compact urban areas in Victoria, with very few vacant allotments south of Reilly Street.

In any case, it was generally understood that it was in the interests of councillors (as property owners themselves) to avoid unnecessary rate increases. Indeed, this was a common reason for electing men of substance to office. As shown in the table below, councillors in East Collingwood (as elsewhere) were drawn chiefly from the largest ratepayers in the district.

Net annual value 1864	*E. C'wood councillors 1855–65* (%)
£100 and above	66
£50 — £99	9
£25 — £49	16
Under £25	9

The left-hand column uses the same categories as the government's survey of 1866; to construct the right-hand column, the present writer compiled a list of the thirty-nine councillors elected between October 1855 and August 1865 and then searched the earliest surviving ratebook (1864) from cover to cover, tallying each councillor's property holdings on a card. Nobody was surprised when, early in 1864, the council rejected a motion to increase the rates from 1s 3d in the pound to 1s 6d.

In the 1860s the science of civic economics was as underdeveloped as the science of medicine. When a municipality's financial affairs appeared to be in a state of chronic disease, the orthodox prescription was profuse blood-letting and occasional amputation. This meant advocating a minimum rate, and 'economizing' on expenditure. Consequently, municipal services, such as street cleaning, had to be curtailed, and the salaries of council staff had to be depressed. The salaries of the town clerk and the surveyor in East Collingwood were usually only two-thirds of those paid in Fitzroy. Particularly during economic depressions, junior officers (the inspector of nuisances and the overseer of works) might be dismissed and their positions amalgamated. 'Economizers' also tended to consider it wasteful to finance prosecutions against persons who broke sanitary laws. These policies endeared economizers to many ratepayers, particularly the wealthiest. 'The holders of large properties', said the *Observer*

> as a rule are not the most energetic for improvements. It is among this class that a minimum rate finds its advocates. The situations they enjoy are generally on main roads, in high and dry localities. The improvements, which are of the greatest consequence to their less fortunate neighbours, are to them frequently a matter of indifference.[5]

During the 1860s a precedent for departing from the orthodoxy of economizing was set in Fitzroy. In 1862 Fitzroy Council obtained a £5,000 loan for kerbing and channelling its streets. The loan proposal caused fierce controversy at first. The case given for the loan was that it would add to the health and comfort of all Fitzroy and, by encouraging more population and trade, would also add to the district's wealth. 'Economizers' objected that the council should not get into debt and that it should finance street works out of the ordinary revenue. The loan project proved to be highly successful. The loan money was spent in 1863, and was repaid from rates in five years. Of Fitzroy's 21 miles of streets in 1866, 19 miles had been metalled, and 15 miles had been kerbed and channelled. The rise of Fitzroy's property values was widely attributed to the loan. The success of the loan converted many of its former opponents, including some in Fitzroy Council.

The *Observer*, in editorials urging the building of a Fitzroy town hall, remarked in 1863 that, for several reasons, Fitzroy was 'rapidly taking foremost place among suburban municipalities'. Firstly, Fitzroy's location—being high, dry and convenient—made it 'a most desirable place of residence to all whose business lies in the metropolis'. Secondly, blessed with ample municipal funds, Fitzroy Council had now almost completed all the necessary public works, and the only major thing still lacking was a proper system of cleansing. Fitzroy was 'fast approaching that happy period when . . . the only charge upon the rates will be maintenance and lighting'. Thirdly, the paper said, Fitzroy was 'peculiarly rich' in the number of 'gentlemen who desire to enjoy the honorary distinctions created by society for its leading citizens . . . Probably in no other suburban borough are so many justices of the peace to be found; while every other mark of honor or respect is eagerly contended for by numerous competitors'. (Fitzroy's residents in-

63

cluded members of parliament, for example. They found Fitzroy convenient to Parliament House.)

During 1864 citizens and councillors in Fitzroy and East Collingwood continually commented on the glaring contrast between the two municipalities. In Fitzroy, it was noted, there was scarcely a house to let. Brick houses were being let even while they were in course of erection. In East Collingwood, however, property was said to be depreciating fast because of the bad drainage and the dilapidated state of the district. Houses were difficult, even impossible, to let. New tenants left disgusted after a week. Consequently rents were falling.

When (as mentioned earlier) the East Collingwood Council was reconstituted and enlarged late in 1864, the mood of the new council was one of urgency. The public notion about East Collingwood (that if the poor went there, they could obtain free soup and houses) had to be corrected. One of the new council's first decisions was to cease financially supporting the Collingwood Soup Kitchen.

The new council took a fresh look at improvement plans. During his election campaign, one councillor had summed up the new mood when he said that East Collingwood ought to rise out of the mud without further delay and that, if money could not be had from the government, there would have to be a special rate.

Estimating the cost of improvement works at £20,000, the council in 1865 decided to obtain a loan of £15,000 (at 8 per cent interest), to be repaid over ten years by drastically increasing the municipal rates from 1s 3d in the pound to 1s 8d. The new rate meant that, though East Collingwood was among the poorest communities in Victoria, it was now one of the most heavily taxed. Fitzroy, for example, increased its rates by only a penny in 1867 (to a total of 1s 4d) and was able to provide more services than East Collingwood.

As will be explained fully in chapter 6, the new council was particularly interested in attracting industrial development on the Flat as a means of increasing local land values. The *Observer* commented on the loan:

> The drainage of the Flat must materially enhance the value of the property there, and the many pieces of vacant ground, now useless, will be speedily built upon . . . There is an evident desire among the East Collingwood councillors to encourage the establishment of manufactories in their district, and a proper system of drainage will remove whatever ill effects could arise from such.[6]

The Highbury Barn Hotel, Hoddle Street, Collingwood (Portion 87); watercolour, about 1854.

The Yarra about 1850, showing John Hodgson's punt crossing between Collingwood and Kew at Clarke Street, near today's Convent of the Good Shepherd.

Galloway Arms Hotel, Johnston Street, Collingwood (Portion 73) ; water-colour by Henry Gritten, 1856.

The Independent Chapel, Oxford Street, Collingwood (Portion 52), now demolished; stone engraving by S. T. Gill, about 1854.

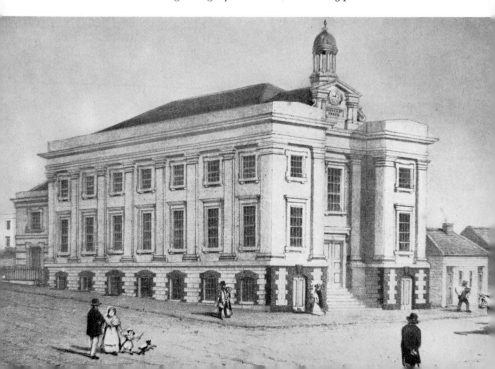

In order to emphasize drainage as well as mere traffic improvement, the council decided to put two of the three new drainage lines (in the north) underground. Some northern ratepayers (in Portions 80 and 87) suspected that this was another southern trick, and for weeks the merits of underground versus surface drainage were debated earnestly like Protection and Free Trade. The underground drains, constructed in 1867, proved to be highly successful. They were egg-shaped, in strong cemented brickwork, measuring 7 ft by 5 ft at their largest point. They had a drop of 1 ft in 250, compared with 1 in 300 in the old Reilly Street open drain. A century later these underground drains are still in use.

In order to transform Elizabeth Street into Langridge Street (the modified Route Q), the council purchased forty-seven properties, including thirty houses. The widening of Gipps Street involved purchasing seventeen properties, including eight houses. These streets, said the local press afterwards, would now be 'more desirable to live in'.

During the arguments of the 1860s about streets running east-west across the Flat, there were also arguments about streets running north-south along the Slope. Two thoroughfares—Wellington Street and Smith Street—were competing for supremacy, with victory finally going to Smith Street.

When the first subdivision on the Slope (Portions 52, 53, 68 and 73) was made in 1849, Wellington Street was laid out as its main axis, with Smith Street forming merely the western boundary. In the 1850s Wellington Street was East Collingwood's most densely populated, and busiest, street. Shop sites there were more sought after—and fetched higher prices—than those in Smith Street. But Wellington Street's business was purely local, because, until the 1870s, it was a short street, blocked off from the growing country trade (from Heidelberg, Northcote and Preston), which proceeded along Smith Street and became absorbed in Fitzroy. From the late 1850s Wellington Street businessmen advocated the extension of Wellington Street through the private land in Portions 81 and 86 and through the Crown lands of Clifton Hill to connect with Heidelberg Road.

In 1859 the council began pressing the government to reserve space for Wellington Street in the Crown lands. The owner of Ryrie's Paddock (swampy Portion 86) donated to the council a strip of land through his paddock, on the condition that the council would finance the construction. (The owner realized that a busy thoroughfare would transform his swamp into marketable building sites.) The remaining obstacle was Portion 81, an early subdivision whose components were now scattered among various owners. The council began approaching these with a view to buying them out, but was hampered throughout the 1860s by lack of funds.

In the council the cause of Wellington Street was advocated by the councillors from the Slope. The *Observer* remarked sarcastically, 'Wellington Street must be opened up to Heidelberg Road because Councillor Petherick's cottages do not let.' The Wellington Street interest was resisted by councillors from the Flat and from the riverside.

As well as wishing to extend Wellington Street, the traders of the Slope (including those in the council) also wanted the government to subdivide and sell the Clifton Hill Crown lands, so that a population (i.e., potential customers) could be built up there. Some Collingwood people were shopping in Melbourne, because they were so close to the city. The future population of Clifton Hill, it was thought, would shop in Collingwood. The government began selling the Clifton Hill lands in 1864, and by the late 1860s Clifton Hill residents were demanding street improvements.

While the Wellington Street extension was in abeyance during the 1860s, the traders of Smith Street were becoming increasingly ambitious, particularly in view of the rapid development of Fitzroy. After making such progress with kerbing and channelling in 1862–5, Fitzroy Council was able to begin constructing, or subsidizing, footpaths of flagstones (flat slabs of rock) in the main streets on the Hill. Not to be outdone, East Collingwood Council decided in 1865 to flag the eastern side of Smith Street, although Fitzroy had not flagged the western side. The case for flagging Smith Street was that it would be a good investment because, unlike gravel, it was permanent; it would benefit Smith Street businessmen and would encourage them to improve some of the old buildings; after Smith Street was completed, the council could then consider streets running off it. The flagging decision was fiercely opposed by councillors from the Flat. East Collingwood, said the Flat, was still too poor to undertake such a luxury; Fitzroy had started its existence with large funds which poor East Collingwood did not have; while flagging was desirable, the kerbing and channelling of the Flat was more urgent and was not yet completed; it was unfair to leave the Flat dwellers suffering in the meanwhile; the council could benefit the Smith Street shopkeepers much more by improving the Flat, thereby increasing the population and potential customers. As it turned out, flagging in Smith Street was left to individual shopkeepers until the council took over, and completed, the task in 1874.

In 1877 the council finally completed opening up Wellington Street to the north. But, by then, Smith Street had replaced Wellington Street as Collingwood's commercial centre. Smith Street, together with Fitzroy's Brunswick Street, was even rivalling Melbourne's central business district.

The notion of civic improvement involved improving people's minds as well as their environment. East Collingwood had increasing need for a venue for public meetings, recreation and culture. From the beginning this need was met by two kinds of private institution, the church and the pub, with the latter receiving greater patronage.

From 1853 to 1864 East Collingwood had one substantial church building (the Independent Chapel in Oxford Street, Portion 52), as well as several small wooden chapels operated by various denominations. It is interesting to trace the development of, say, Anglicanism as a case study in the role of organized religion there. In the 1850s East Collingwood did not even count as an Anglican parish, but was part of the parish of St Mark's Church, Fitzroy, which flourished on elevated Portion 69. Some traders from the East Collingwood Slope attended St Mark's, but working folk from the Flat were deterred by the need to pay pew-rents (a normal charge in middle-class suburbs) and to wear good clothes. Charles Baker, a printing compositor who was a prominent Anglican layman in East Collingwood, denounced the pew-rent system in Melbourne church newspapers.

In 1855 a wealthy Anglican layman, John Matthew Smith, donated some land on swampy Portion 65, on which a schoolroom was built, with a full-time schoolmaster. From 1858 onwards the schoolroom was also used for Anglican religious services, conducted by a layman, Nathaniel Kinsman, who was a Fitzroy secondhand furniture dealer. When the Church of England decided to appoint an ordained minister to East Collingwood in 1862, Kinsman and his congregation objected to the appointment. They seceded and erected a 'Free Church of England' nearby (with, according to census reports, 111 adherents in 1871 and 51 in 1881). Henceforth, Kinsman's position as 'minister' enabled him to build up a lucrative business as an officiator at 'quick and cheap' weddings—a total of 9,800 weddings in thirty-four years, usually conducted at his

Fitzroy auction rooms, in between sales of pieces of furniture.

After the schism, loyal Anglicans proceeded to erect a bluestone church, St Philip's, on swampy Portion 66 for the new parish of East Collingwood. In an editorial marking the founding in 1864, the *Observer* commented that the loyalists had had to surmount a difficulty peculiar to East Collingwood—'the comparative absence of a wealthy class' there. East Collingwood's population, it said, was 'especially of that kind which most needs well organized clerical aid, and at the same time is the least likely to make any personal sacrifices to obtain it'—meaning apparently pew-rents and other offerings. The editorial (written during the long delay in implementing an East Collingwood drainage project) added that the founding of St Philip's in the middle of the Flat was a milestone in the improvement of the Flat:

> [It] raises hopes in the hearts of all who are interested in the moral and social welfare of the population. When East Collingwood numbers in her midst well educated and untiring citizens, with some degree of leisure, it will not be long before their attention will be turned to the abominable disgrace of civic affairs as at present conducted, and, remembering that cleanliness is next to godliness, organize the population to thoroughly drain, cleanse and improve the borough.

A century later, in 1969, when parish life at St Philip's had come to a standstill because of social changes in Collingwood, diocesan authorities demolished the bluestone church, despite pleas by the National Trust that it should be preserved for its historical value.

Meanwhile, for most Collingwood men, the main place for meeting and for spending leisure was the pub. Here, one need neither reserve a seat nor dress up. Countless lodges, friendly societies, sporting bodies, working men's clubs and ratepayers' groups met at their favourite hotels. The better hotels provided a special meeting room. These gatherings were part of an oral, face-to-face culture. Compared with churches, they have left few relics but their role in Victoria's history is no less significant. Functions held at these hotels included the meetings of the first East Collingwood and Fitzroy Councils (until council chambers were built), rallies for important social movements (including the agitation for land reform, for the eight-hour day, and for tariff protection), and election rallies for the municipal councils and for the Legislative Assembly. East Collingwood Council always included at least one publican, though never a clergyman.

In 1866, when St Philip's Church was newly opened, East Collingwood had sixty licensed liquor houses. Licences were granted (or renewed or transferred) cheaply and indiscriminately without much reference, if any, to the standard of building, accommodation, comfort, liquor or the licensee's character. Two-thirds of the buildings were assessed at the low net annual value of between £35 and £70; only one-quarter exceeded £100. The existence of low-standard rookeries was said to force down standards even in the better hotels. In 1879 there were ninety-eight liquor licences (eighty-seven hotels, eleven wine and spirit merchants)—that is, one licensed trader to each hundred adults. The figures for Fitzroy then were similar, and the local press complained that the hotel trade in both municipalities had 'dwindled to the mere selling of intoxicating drinks'.

From the early 1850s, thoughtful citizens in both Fitzroy and East Collingwood advocated facilities for adult education in the form of a mechanics' institute providing books, lectures, concerts and debates. A mechanics' institute, it was said, would counteract indolence, drunkenness, vice and crime, and would contribute to the improvement of the district. In 1856 the government decided that, as the two municipalities constituted one electorate, it would grant £500 towards a joint institute. With this sum, land in Smith Street (Portion 68, on the East Collingwood side) was bought and was vested in a trust of prominent citizens. However, public subscriptions proved to be insufficient to erect a building. For the time being, mechanics' institute gatherings were held at the Oxford Street Independent Chapel (e.g., a lecture by industrialist Thomas Rae on 'The Progress of the Industrial Classes').

Both East Collingwood and Fitzroy Councils declined to contribute towards the construction of a joint institute on the Smith Street site. Fitzroy Council preferred not to spend money outside its own boundary line, and East Collingwood Council objected to another council having any power within East Collingwood. In 1860, while the Faction X councillors from the Johnston Street area were in control, East Collingwood Council established instead a free library in its new municipal building in Johnston Street in Portion 73.

The question of what should be done with the Smith Street site raised itself again in the mid-1860s. For one thing, Smith Street was developing as Collingwood's major commercial street. Furthermore, agitation in Collingwood for industrial development and for shorter working hours was increasing the need and scope for adult education. The local press looked forward to a time when,

69

in a well-conducted institute, 'the well-woven lecture may await the young man, at leisure from the early closing movement'. The Early Closing Association itself asked the council to keep the Johnston Street municipal library open until later in the evening—11 o'clock.

In 1865 the government offered to grant £3,500 towards the erection of a building on the Smith Street site, costing £5,000 and containing a mechanics' institute and post office, providing that the two councils contributed £750 each. The plan was welcomed by prominent citizens in both municipalities, but was eventually rejected by Fitzroy Council under pressure from businessmen of Brunswick Street, the main street of Fitzroy. It was feared that Brunswick Street, which already had a post office of its own, would lose trade and prestige to Smith Street. Fitzroy Council unsuccessfully sought to have the Collingwood electorate divided, alleging that the three members of parliament were controlled by votes from the eastern municipality.

The Collingwood-Fitzroy *Manufacturer* suggested that one barrier to a joint mechanics' institute was clannishness and snobbery on Fitzroy's part. The paper criticized Fitzroy firemen for having refused recently to attend a fire in Wellington Street, East Collingwood. It also condemned 'the childish absurdity of speaking of the Flattites as inferior to, and behind, the inhabitants of Fitzroy'. East Collingwood, it said, deserved to 'share in the benefits of that culture that ever rebounds where it penetrates', for 'in the institute we all meet on one footing. Intellect and culture are the true communists [i.e., levellers]'. The paper urged Fitzroy: 'Embrace, then, this opportunity of . . . doing your duty to your neighbour.' One big hall and one big library, it said, were better than two small halls and two small libraries: 'There may the ratepayer of Fitzroy sit by the side of him of East Collingwood, no longer severed by clannish mistrust, but blest and blessing in the generous rivalry of which district shall produce the best musicians and orators.' The paper even suggested complete amalgamation of the two municipalities: 'Who would not welcome the day that sees the two districts united into one borough . . . One council, one staff of local functionaries, and one feeling of common interest and of common progress!'

Finally, in 1867, the government decided to vest the Smith Street site in the East Collingwood Council. In return, the council reserved portion of the site for a government post office; on the remainder, the council erected a mechanics' institute, later named the Royal Albert Institute. Fitzroy councillors protested about the government favouring East Collingwood. The *Manufacturer* alleged that one of these councillors was himself an unsuccessful tenderer for the contract to erect the building.

Meanwhile, Fitzroy Council was turning its thoughts towards the erection of a grand town hall and public library, to be financed by a public loan. Long arguments ensued about which street was to be favoured as the site; and there was a facetious suggestion that the town hall be erected on wheels and be shifted from time to time as the centre of the town changed. Opened in 1874, Fitzroy Town Hall was one of the first 'boom-style' halls that rose in suburb after suburb during the next two decades. Collingwood's town hall opened a decade later than Fitzroy's but was bigger.

SANITATION AND POLLUTION

from cesspits to cesspans

In the nineteenth-century metropolis, concern about sanitation and pollution was usually delayed until two conditions existed: when accumulations of sewage, garbage, junk and air pollution could no longer be ignored by eyes and noses; and when there was a scare about miasma and epidemics.

During the gold immigration of 1852–3, a parliamentary committee on sanitation was horrified at the accumulations of filth around Melbourne, and said that Melbourne's relative immunity from epidemic was merely due to the graciousness of providence. In 1854 Alexander K. Smith, a Gas Company engineer living on the Slope at East Collingwood, wrote an essay about Melbourne's sanitary condition, commenting:

> After the cholera had visited Europe and the British Isles in 1853, plans of towns and cities were coloured, showing where the frightful visitor had been most destructive. There would be little difficulty in preparing a plan of Melbourne distinctly pointing out those places that would number the most victims if ever that terrible scourge came amongst us.[1]

Smith said that refuse heaps, 'lying decomposing before the doors and under the windows of sleeping rooms', emitted 'gases which spread disease and death into the lungs of the careless and ignorant inhaler'.

In 1855 the Victorian government established the Central Board of Health, which reported that the absence of sanitation in metropolitan Melbourne 'leaves the decomposition of animal and vegetable matter to accumulate, by evaporation, in the atmosphere, which nothing but the natural salubrity of the climate prevents from causing a vast amount of disease'. The formation of the Central Board of Health represented a slight improvement. Apart from its full-time chairman, the Board employed a full-time itinerant inspector with civil engineering qualifications, who annually visited all major towns and suburbs. Under the Public Health Act, each local council employed an inspector of nuisances (usually a local police sergeant in the 1850s, but a regular full-time council officer thereafter), and retained a local medical practitioner as part-time health officer.

The usual impulse in tackling the problem of waste disposal was to shift the refuse (and the problem) to somewhere else. Take, for example, the question of garbage and other rubbish. Normally, householders threw organic garbage into backyards, to be trodden underfoot or sifted by domestic animals—dogs, poultry, goats, cows and pigs. Pigs, because they not only got rid of garbage but also turned it into meat, were popular in establishments that had much garbage or needed much meat—butchers' shops, hotels and lodging houses. For example, a butcher would keep a pig to dispose of offal, and would eventually slaughter the pig for pork. In the late 1850s and early 1860s the Central Board of Health reminded local councils that the Public Health Act prohibited the keeping of pigs near dwellings. The law was enforced in Emerald Hill (South Melbourne) in 1860, but was ignored in East Collingwood, apart from the occasional prosecution of butchers. In 1862 East Collingwood Council by four votes to three rejected a motion to prohibit the keeping of pigs within the municipality. The four pro-pig councillors considered the action 'too sweeping and despotic'. One of the other three said that he supported the motion because he had now fattened his pig and was about to sell it. The biggest concentration of pigs in East Collingwood was at a butcher's piggery near the East Collingwood abattoirs in Ramsden Street, Clifton Hill, beside the Merri Creek. The pigs wallowed in unpaved yards; their food, scattered about promiscuously in the mud, comprised offal from the abattoirs (sometimes including a whole carcass, which remained there until reduced to a skeleton).

Refuse not consumed by animals (such as ashes, animal manure, carcasses and junk) used to accumulate in backyards until the occupier dumped it in the nearest street channel, back lane, vacant allotment or swamp. Beginning in 1857, whenever dead animals (dogs, goats, pigs, etc.) accumulated in alleys and vacant allotments, East Collingwood Council would engage a contractor to remove them for about 1s 6d each. The council posted notices and distributed handbills, warning of a fine of up to £20 for dumping dead animals, broken bottles, and other rubbish, but this failed to discourage the practice. In 1861, following an epidemic, the council sent scavenger carts to remove the accumulated refuse from streets, but did not adopt a suggestion that this should be a regular service twice a week. A favourite dumping place was a swamp at the northern end of Smith Street in Portion 85. The refuse there, said the Collingwood *Observer*, included 'dead fowls, goats and animals of all sorts, differing in size from a rat to a cow'. These carcasses were sifted by pigs, and became 'fermented, then tramped upon and mashed by the unfortunate cows depastured in the neighbourhood, till all substance has been destroyed and rank decomposition poisons the air'. Another dumping place was the open drain along Reilly Street, where refuse included 'stones, dead cats, and pots and pans'. Consequently the drain often became blocked and overflowed into Collingwood streets.

Alexander Smith, in the essay referred to earlier, noted that, compared with other parts of the world, Melbourne's litter included an unusually large accumulation of rubbish (bones, rags, old garments, boots, bagging and wrapping), as distinct from organic garbage. Because of Victoria's comparatively high living standards, he said, collecting and dealing in junk was a less attractive and less pressing occupation here than elsewhere.

As urbanization and industrialization proceeded, the range of non-edible rubbish (e.g., cardboard, bottles, cans) increased, making the pig a less versatile consumer; and suitable dumping places became scarce. Advanced thinkers like Alexander Smith advocated that, instead of having to dump, householders should be encouraged to maintain a garbage receptacle—'a dust bin', preferably with a lid—which would be emptied regularly by the municipality. Smith suggested that bones and other animal refuse could be converted into charcoal for later use as a deodorizing agent. In 1864 Fitzroy became one of the first municipalities in Australia to establish a municipal garbage collection service, preceding even the City of Melbourne. Fitzroy's service was fortnightly, at sixpence a time, and was optional. 'It must be made imperative', said the *Observer*, 'if it is to meet the most objectionable cases.'

The Fitzroy example was soon followed by the municipality of Hotham (North Melbourne), but many Australian towns waited for another decade or more. The municipal council of Brisbane, for example, introduced a garbage collection service in 1875.

In Fitzroy and on the East Collingwood Slope, kerbing and channelling facilitated the sweeping and flushing of streets. On the Flat, however, the streets merely had ditches (called 'earth channels'). Unsweepable, these were receptacles for garbage and sewage, and were not reconstructed with stone until the mid-1870s. In 1864, as well as its garbage service, Fitzroy Council also had squads of labourers with drays, engaged constantly on sweeping streets, channels and alleys. With up to eleven sweepers and garbage collectors, Fitzroy spent about £900 a year. East Collingwood had about five labourers and spent £7 a week—or theoretically about £400 a year, but East Collingwood was notorious for dismissing its labourers when funds were short. In 1865 both councils changed from day labour to contract in order to cut cleaning costs. A contractor could use his sons as cheap labour and could sell the street sweepings for a shilling a load as agricultural fertilizer. East Collingwood Council hoped that its dismissed labourers would be among the tenderers and would compete for the privilege of working for less money. Under the contract system, Fitzroy still spent about £650 a year in 1866 and 1867. In East Collingwood, residents and some councillors continued to complain about dirty streets, with rubbish accumulating in heaps.

The biggest sanitary problem for the metropolis was the disposal of night-soil, and it is necessary to outline this problem in order to present a full picture of the suburban scene.

In the mid-nineteenth century privy out-houses in Australia were usually constructed over or near a cesspit. Cesspits were of varying degrees of sophistication. In the 1850s and 1860s the typical cesspit on Collingwood Flat tended to be at the primitive end of the scale—a mere hole dug in the ground. It was probably never emptied; when it became filled with solid matter, it might be covered over with earth, and the timber superstructure would be moved a few yards away to a new hole. On the Slope and in southern Fitzroy, where dense settlement made portability less possible, the cesspit might be constructed of blocks of bluestone but was probably not made watertight. This cesspit was often made larger so that it might less often require emptying, and generally was emptied only when absolutely necessary. In Fitzroy the altitude and the nature of the soil permitted the liquid contents of the cesspit to percolate into the ground and to gravitate downhill towards the Flat. Indeed, some cesspits were fitted with a pipe for conveying (or even for deliberately flushing) the liquid overflow into the street channel—and downhill. The overflow pipe was particularly necessary where 'water closets' existed; these tended to be in double-storey buildings, which meant Fitzroy and the

Slope rather than the Flat. The cesspits on the Flat, therefore, tended to collect not only sewage from the Flat but also soakage and drainage from the higher areas. Often the contents, augmented by rainwater, overflowed around, and even under, buildings. Perhaps more than anything else, this fact conveys the horrors of life on Collingwood Flat.

The two municipalities differed in their attitudes to cesspit standards. East Collingwood Council rejected a motion in 1857 for a by-law regulating the standard. After the alarming increase in East Collingwood mortality in 1860–1, the Central Board of Health pointed to the municipality's need for watertight cesspits. The Board also circulated designs for pits made from a cask (preferably pitched and tarred on the outside) for thirty shillings or from bricks (preferably lined with cement) for £3. A sound oak barrel, it was said, might last fifteen years or more. East Collingwood Council did not bother to propagate these designs in the district, although some residents did adopt them voluntarily over the years. Fitzroy Council, on the other hand, immediately conducted a campaign. Within a year it succeeded in securing the construction of 'a large number of these receptacles', and received praise from the Board. Fitzroy then passed a by-law making the watertight pits compulsory, although the government refused to endorse such a by-law until legislation was passed in 1867. Meanwhile, many of Fitzroy's supposedly watertight cesspits, even if properly lined with tar or cement, deteriorated over the years and again became like a sewer, through which the fluid percolated into the ground.

In the late 1850s several nightmen were paying a small annual licence fee to each suburban council for the right to empty cesspits in the municipality, but they had to find clients for themselves, not through the council. The nightmen were not yet achieving the full potential of trade. Landlords and tenants often disputed their individual liability of payment for the nightman's services (about 7s 6d a cartload in the 1860s). Cesspits commonly continued to overflow until the council's inspector of nuisances issued an order, or even a summons. In East Collingwood such coercion was rare, and conviction was even more so. The council and the local justices regarded cesspits as a bona fide nuisance. Even the chairman of Fitzroy Council's health committee admitted that his privy had not been emptied for years, having always been absorbed by the surrounding ground. As early as 1855, an astute nightman recommended East Collingwood Council to follow the example of some English towns in establishing a universal compulsory night-soil collection service, to be financed from a special rate (from £1 a year for a small dwelling to £4 for a hotel). Not surprisingly the rate-conscious East Collingwood Council was unmoved. A compulsory special rate for such a purpose was unprecedented in Victoria, and was not legal until 1890, although a few councils supported a nightman's service out of general rates in the 1870s. The Central Board of Health, which pressed the government for thirty years for such legislation, had places like East Collingwood in mind when it pointed out that so long as the maintenance of cleanliness in cesspools was left to individuals, it would not be carried out where it was most needed—in the crowded dwellings of the 'poorer classes'.

The removal of refuse from settled areas created the problem of where to dump it. Thus arose the institution called 'manure depot'—a kind of communal cesspit situated on Crown or municipal land on the fringes of settlement, near enough to town for convenience, yet far enough away for comfort. In the mid-1850s, night-soil from East Collingwood and Fitzroy went to the City of Melbourne manure depot in Flemington Road, Royal Park, on the city's northern fringe. From there, according to the original plan, the refuse was to be sold to farmers and gardeners. Even after deducting operating expenses, a profit was expected for the city coffers.

In practice, however, the process of urbanization worked against this plan. Population growth resulted in an increased production of night-soil but suburban sprawl decreased the number of potential consumers, especially those prepared to pay for a product in oversupply. By the mid-1860s more than two hundred loads of night-soil a week were being dumped at Royal Park but, as this consisted chiefly of liquid matter, the proportion suitable for agricultural purposes was small. The depot cost £300 to £400 a year to operate, but earned less than £50 a year from sale of manure.

Another problem was that, although the Royal Park manure depot was at first remote from houses, settlement gradually crept out towards it, and an increasing stream of fetid drainage ran from the depot within range of the new houses. In 1861, therefore, Melbourne City Council prohibited other municipalities from using the depot, and told them to set up depots of their own.

The Central Board of Health, anxious to avoid the multiplication of depots, advocated the establishment of a general depot, serving Melbourne, East Collingwood, Fitzroy and Hotham. However, the scheme was doomed because of disagreement among municipalities. East Collingwood in 1861 obtained a grant of Crown land on the Merri Creek at Clifton Hill for a depot of its own, and erected buildings worth £500. East Collingwood Council declined to consider the advantage of co-operative action or to accept financial assistance from other municipalities. As in the case of the proposed joint mechanics' institute (see p. 69), the council objected to any other council exercising power within East Collingwood. After the East Collingwood depot began operating, the council skimped on operating costs (wages and deodorizing chemicals), and this depot eventually degenerated like the Royal Park one.

After East Collingwood's defection, a general depot for the other three municipalities was proposed in Macaulay Road, Hotham. Precipitation tanks and filtering apparatus were to be used (as in England) to extract sewage solids for conversion into agricultural manure. Liquid residue was to be used to fertilize the nearby Flemington swamp, which would be sold as market gardens. However, Hotham Council, fearing nuisances, rejected the scheme, although it proceeded to use the Macaulay Road site as its own depot. The C.B.H. decided to revert to the original Royal Park site. Because the passage of nightcarts from Fitzroy through Carlton would be a nuisance within the City of Melbourne, Melbourne City Council now objected to the inclusion of Fitzroy in the plan, even though Fitzroy was willing to enforce a roundabout route.

Meanwhile, Dr Richard T. Tracy, Fitzroy municipal health officer, had devised a system for filtering hospital sewage through a bed of bluestone metal, charcoal and oyster shells, making the drainage 'inoffensive' enough to be allowed into the street channels. Impressed, the C.B.H. suggested a joint depot, using this process, for East Collingwood and Fitzroy, but East Collingwood declined. Next, Fitzroy Council proposed a depot of its own on Crown land on the Merri Creek at North Fitzroy, but this was opposed by the government, which still feared a multiplication of depots, and by North Fitzroy residents, who feared a nuisance. Exasperated, Dr Tracy commented in 1864:

> I very much fear it will require an epidemic to arouse the attention of the authorities to this very important matter . . . The fault does not lie in Fitzroy. It is the difficulty of getting larger bodies to move with us, and the desire on the part of the central authorities to have a depot on a grand scale, that has prevented our being allowed to provide for our own wants.[2]

Late in 1864, when at last some agreement was effected between

Fitzroy, Melbourne and Hotham, the new Royal Park works proved to be inadequate, but the government refused further funds. By 1866 neither the Royal Park nor East Collingwood manure depots could cope with more night-soil. Yet about eighty cartloads a week were still being removed from the cesspits of Collingwood-Fitzroy and another sixty cartloads from Carlton-Hotham, as well as much more from the city proper.

Manure depots were not the only outlet for Collingwood-Fitzroy night-soil. Some nightmen (particularly in Fitzroy) lightened their load into street channels, along roadways or on vacant allotments. Both councils paid rewards (usually to policemen) for information leading to the conviction of offenders. Fitzroy Council was particularly conscientious. Whereas East Collingwood's reward in the early 1860s was 10s, Fitzroy's rose to £5 in 1866, although it was reduced to £2 and then £1 in 1867.

By 1864 the bulk of the night-soil collected from Fitzroy, and probably from East Collingwood also, was being emptied into the River Yarra at Johnston Street bridge, transforming the Yarra into Melbourne's biggest cesspool—a flowing manure depot. As the *Observer* commented, 'the river is thus poisoned and the water rendered impure, which—whenever one of those frequent accidents occur to the Yan Yean main—becomes the only drinking water for these two important boroughs.' Two methods were used at the bridge. One was described by Fitzroy town clerk W. J. Gilchrist at a parliamentary inquiry in 1866:

> It [the night-soil] is poured off Johnston Street bridge . . . There is a difficulty of proving it, because men are on the watch; but I have been told, in fact, by nightmen, that such has been the case . . . They put the hose from the cart over the rail of the bridge.
>
> QUESTION: Is there any peculiarity as to the police division in the bridge?
>
> ANSWER: I think East Collingwood ends with the commencement of the bridge, and the other division commences at the other end, and it is No-man's-land in the centre.[3]

The second method, referred to later in this chapter, was a more institutionalized one, which developed at the end of the 1860s: nightmen poured night-soil down the banks of the Yarra beside the bridge by arrangement with a market gardener there.

In 1852, when settlement was just beginning to spread beyond the municipal boundary of Melbourne into East Collingwood, a select committee of the Legislative Council considered a scheme for sewering central Melbourne. The scheme provided for pipes for house drainage, emptying into the Yarra in the city below Queen's wharf and costing £120,000 (or much more if the outfall were extended further downstream near the junction with the Saltwater, or Maribyrnong, River). The sudden suburban sprawl over the Collingwood-Richmond Flat increased the technical problems, and cost, of sewerage. Not only did the Flat lack natural gravitation, but its haphazard development meant that any sewerage lines there would have to take a roundabout route, passing countless vacant allotments not immediately needing sewerage. Even so, the Central Board of Health later estimated from English experience that the principal and interest required for sewering Melbourne and the four inner municipalities (East Collingwood, Richmond, Fitzroy and Hotham) could be paid off in thirty years by a rate costing householders less than the sum required for properly maintaining cesspits. The Central Board's reasoning was that the five municipalities had about 15,000 cesspits; to make these watertight would cost £60,000; to empty them properly would entail a perpetual tax of £15,000 a year. During the 1860s, enlarged sewerage systems were advocated—for example, one providing for the effluent to be piped to a plant at Fishermen's Bend below Melbourne where it would be deodorized and filtered, the solids to be dried and manufactured into manure, and the fluid to irrigate sandy flats near the Yarra's mouth.

The sewerage question was complicated by conflicts of interest between the various civic authorities that developed in the metropolitan area after 1855—the original but shrinking City of Melbourne, the new proliferating suburban municipalities and the government-appointed Sewerage and Water Commission. As explained in chapter 4, East Collingwood, for example, became committed in 1866 to its own system of underground storm-water drains, which in that water-logged municipality seemed of more pressing importance than the niceties of household sewerage. Sewerage was of greater appeal to the City of Melbourne, which was downstream from the river pollution emanating from Collingwood. And there were differences of opinion about the degrees of authority that would be exercised by the City Council and the Sewerage Commission in a sewerage system.

By the beginning of 1866 it could no longer be ignored that the night-soil problem was a metropolitan one, rather than a local municipal one, and that it required a uniform metropolitan solu-

tion. That year several circumstances influenced the various councils to relax their usual aggressive independence temporarily and
to enter into joint negotiations.

Firstly, in October 1865 came news of a cholera epidemic in
Europe. Whereas deaths from typhoid were accepted as normal
wastage (as traffic accidents are today), cholera frightened because
it was not normally present in Australia or even in Europe. 'This
is certainly most important news', said the *Observer*, 'and will
affect us materially even at this part of the world . . . The memory
of the effect of cholera in 1830, and again in later years, makes us
shudder at the consequences, if it should break out in Victoria.'
The paper expected that 'the next mail will bring to many a Victorian home the intelligence of the death of those left behind in
the old country'. According to miasma theory, the paper said,

> cholera is an epidemic conveyed by an atmospheric agency; if so, then
> there is no part of the world actually safe from the visit of such a
> dreadful scourge. There can be no doubt, however, that the more
> cleanly a district or country is kept, the less likelihood is there for such
> being made the abode of this unwelcome visitor.

Otherwise, the only hope was that in Victoria 'our balmy air, our
salubrious climate, and, above all, the hot wind, may suppress the
germination of the noxious poison if ever it reaches us'.

Secondly, early in 1866 the sewerage question came to a practical
issue when the Public Works Department proposed to construct an
underground drain along Elizabeth Street, Melbourne, from the
General Post Office to the Yarra. This proposal prompted Melbourne City Council to invite the co-operation of the government
in a scheme of sewerage intended for the entire metropolis. The
City Council's move alarmed the suburban municipalities. As the
Melbourne *Age* put it:

> They very naturally dread that, in the construction of any general
> scheme, they may be called upon to pay their quota, and they are
> bestirring themselves to lessen some of the evils which have rendered
> drainage desirable, with a view to limit the operation of any scheme
> to the city proper.[4]

Accordingly, in February 1866 a conference was held between
delegates from East Collingwood, Hotham and Richmond Councils. The conference resolved that the city manure depot was a
source of great nuisance to the surrounding districts; that it
was too limited for the requirements of the city and northern
suburbs; that suburban depots for night-soil were undesirable on

sanitary grounds; and that some means should be found of deodorizing night-soil in closets and of facilitating the regular removal of
the deodorized night-soil from populated areas.

But exactly *how* could night-soil be removed from the metropolis? For years before the 1866 conference, various proposals had
been made.

In 1854 Alexander K. Smith, of East Collingwood, to whom we
referred earlier, won £50 offered by Melbourne City Council for
'the best practical plan'. He proposed that night-soil (pumped
from cesspits) should be collected in air-tight carts and should
be floated down the Yarra in air-tight barges to be either converted
into solid manure or dumped in Port Phillip Bay or Bass Strait.

About 1858, sanitation authorities considered plans for removing night-soil from the metropolis by means of the new trunk
railways. One possibility, considered by the Central Board of
Health and the Melbourne City Council, was to use the railways
leading to the goldfields, with a night-soil depot perhaps ten miles
from Melbourne on the Keilor plains. An alternative, favoured
by East Collingwood and Fitzroy councils, was to take over a tramroad, which had been used for transporting water pipes along St
George's Road through North Fitzroy, Northcote and Preston to
Yan Yean during the formation of Melbourne's reticulated water
system. The tramroad, the councils said, could be converted from
wooden rails to iron rails, with either horses or steam locomotives,
for less than £6,000 a mile. The line would open up a future
suburban area to the north of Melbourne, and could be extended
to Kilmore and Seymour in central Victoria. Nightmen, if enabled
to shorten their travelling and to serve more clients, would gladly
pay 2s a load to use the tramroad. Each morning, three or four
truckloads, with iron tanks, could be removed, perhaps by four
horses, to eight or ten miles out of town. The councils envisaged a
central terminal station on about twenty-four acres of land at the
intersection of Nicholson Street and Reilly Street, Fitzroy, and
hoped that, with steam and passengers, this might eventually rival
the existing terminals in Flinders Street and Spencer Street, Melbourne. However, when the other suburban councils considered
the tramroad proposal at their conference in 1866, they discarded
it as being too expensive to implement themselves, and looked
for an easier solution.

The cheap solution that emerged from the 1866 conference was the later famous—or notorious—system of portable pans. The councils recommended that parliament should make pans compulsory and should authorize a rate for systematic emptying. This, they hoped, would indefinitely avoid the expense of suburban sewerage. The government ignored these recommendations. Its 1867 health legislation merely prohibited leaky cesspits, thereby leaving pans optional as an alternative to watertight cesspits.

The kind of pan recommended by the councils (and also by a Parliamentary Select Committee on night-soil in 1866) was an English version called an earth closet, into which dry clay or sand was sprinkled to act as an absorbent and deodorizer. This preoccupation with moisture and odour reflects the influence of the miasmatic theory of disease. Periodically, the earth was to be removed by a nightman (or, according to one early suggestion, emptied on to a garden compost heap). After being dried, the earth could be used again, thereby lessening the accumulation of refuse at manure depots.

The *Observer* endorsed the earth closet, adding it to other important policies such as land reform and protection. Indeed, the manufacture of earth closets became a local industry, conducted by George H. Stanesby, of Fitzroy Street, Fitzroy. His components were a pan, a seat, and scoop for sprinkling earth. His main competitor was D. S. Campbell, a city merchant, who formed a company and patented a 'mechanical' closet—with a hand-lever for sprinkling the earth. Characteristically the *Observer* preferred the local closet to the city one; Campbell's lever, it said, tended to jam. In 1867 an East Collingwood man began manufacturing earth closets, boasting an improved earth-sprinkling apparatus.

The earth closet won some adherents in Fitzroy, and Fitzroy Council officially recommended it to the public. In 1870, when public concern was rising about the prevalence of typhoid fever, the earth closet also received the endorsement of a newly appointed health officer in Fitzroy, Edward Hunt, M.D. Dr Hunt's remarks, which were based not on miasma doctrine but on 'common sense' observation, are worth quoting at length:

> Nothing is known with certainty as to the causes of [the various] forms of fever, and they have been variously ascribed to defective drainage, overcrowding, &c. In Fitzroy defective drainage can hardly be assigned as a cause, its elevated position being so favourable to the flow of surface water. Soakage from cesspools has been assigned as an exciting cause of these forms of fever; I must, however, say that I have not been able to trace this connexion in cases that have come under my notice

. . . But . . . soakage from cesspits . . . is certainly an abominable nuisance and I strongly recommend the adoption of the earth closet system.[5]

East Collingwood Council, however, showed little interest in the earth closet. East Collingwood's role came to be chiefly in maintaining the earth closets of other districts, for in 1869 Thomas Theophilus Draper and Son, nightmen specializing in earth closets, obtained a lease of the East Collingwood Council's manure depot as their headquarters for £25 a year. Draper served about seven hundred earth closets throughout the metropolis, visiting each in daylight hours about three times a week for a charge of £2 10s to £3 a year. At the East Collingwood depot the earth was deodorized (with gas-lime, tar and sulphate of iron), stored until dry, and powdered by machinery for re-use in closets a second and third time. Finally it was sold as garden manure for 10s to £1 a ton. Fluid refuse was carted in casks to a farm owned by Draper at Heidelberg. Draper equipped the depot with a tramway several hundred yards long, costing £150. In some suburbs the earth closet was another household appliance; in East Collingwood it was another industry.

The earth closet had limitations in a poorer suburb like Collingwood. It was the responsibility of the householder to arrange for supplies of suitable clay or sand; and from the outset it was anticipated that 'the poorer classes' would be unlikely to give daily attention to the sprinkling process. East Collingwood health officer Dr A. C. Livingstone told the parliamentary inquiry on night-soil disposal in 1866 that earth closets were suitable where strict supervision existed—for example, he said, in a private residence (meaning a middle-class house in a polite suburb) or in a public institution (where poorer-class inhabitants were under control). But earth closets were unsuitable for 'the general population', especially in a poor and densely populated district like Collingwood where, he said, negligence was more likely.

Subsequent experience confirmed Livingstone's view. 'Quality' nightmen like Draper were undercut by others who emptied an earthless pan for less than half the cost and eventually by councils who made it cheaper still. By the 1880s most pan closets in metropolitan Melbourne were earthless. Brunswick Council's health officer reported in 1887:

The comparative failure of the pan system is due to what we have not at present, a cheap deodorizer or disinfectant; the present disinfectants and deodorizers answer the purpose well, but the price removes them from general use. The rich may use them but the masses will not and do not.

Livingstone, in his 1866 statement, showed insight into long-term implications of night-soil disposal. He predicted that the removal of night-soil from the metropolis in carts (whether from earth closets or from cheaper earthless ones) would become, in the long run, 'the most expensive system imaginable'. He said he supported a plan of the 1850s for constructing a sewer along Collingwood and Richmond flats and then parallel with the Yarra through the City of Melbourne, emptying into the lower Yarra near the junction with the Saltwater (Maribyrnong) River. Sewerage, he said, was more in accord with the interests of East Collingwood people than the earth closet was. For one thing, the cost of sewerage would fall on the owners of property rather than tenants. At the parliamentary inquiry the following exchange took place:

QUESTION: Which do you think would be the greater for East Collingwood—the cost of removing the contents of the closets, or paying, as a perpetual tax, the interest on a very large loan to effect the drainage into the Saltwater River?

LIVINGSTONE: It is worth while to incur the greater expense for the sake of efficiency, and it [sewerage] is a system, of course, that will work forever.

QUESTION: But the expense is a consideration?

LIVINGSTONE: The landlord must put in the water-closets in every house.

QUESTION: That would be a consideration in the rental?

LIVINGSTONE: Of course. If the community put down a sewer system, then I think it should be compulsory to have water-closets; and all the expense of putting them in should be borne by the landlord.

Reading Livingstone's comments, one is reminded of twentieth-century controversies over public and private transport and over public and private education. He saw the issue as a choice between private earth closets, which suited the few, and public sewerage, which suited the many. He indicated that he hardly expected Collingwood's landlords, including those in the council, to be in the vanguard of any public clamour for sewerage.

Despite the earth-closet diversion, the existence of cesspits and earthless closets perpetuated the disposal problem. In the late 1860s both East Collingwood and Fitzroy Councils permitted nightmen (for a fee) to trench night-soil in parkland reserves at

North Fitzroy and Clifton Hill but, because of the increasing population there, this became impracticable in the 1870s.

As mentioned earlier, a market gardener beside the Johnston Street bridge was receiving payment from nightmen in the late 1860s for the right to pour night-soil on the banks of the Yarra there. After the practice had been quietly tolerated for some years, the council tried to discourage the landowner during a clean-up campaign in 1871, but without success. Four years later the Central Board of Health investigated the property and reported:

> The contents of as many as a dozen night-carts were nightly sent into the river, the night-soil being taken to the land in question ostensibly as manure, while in reality it was thrown into a shoot or drain expressly constructed for the purpose of leading it into the river . . . The nightmen willingly paid a fee of two shillings per load for permission to empty their carts so near town, and thus make three or four times as many trips each night.[6]

In one week in March 1875, fifty-two loads were dumped there. This practice was outlawed in 1876 but, as late as 1880, night-soil was allegedly percolating into the Yarra from trenches at the Collingwood night-soil depot.

From this chapter, it will be seen that the evolution of an organized system of removing human waste was gradually shifting the onus from the individual to the community and from the amateur to the professional. At first, cesspits, and even the householder-operated earth closets, were do-it-yourself solutions applied by the unskilled individual householder.

Then, with the growth of the nightman's trade, the solution moved from the level of the individual to the level of the municipality, and called into being semi-skilled practitioners (the nightman and the local council's inspector of nuisances). Finally, sewerage, as we shall see later, was to involve metropolitan, as distinct from municipal, action, and was related to the rise of full-time skilled practitioners—plumbers, civil engineers, industrial chemists and administrators.

Throughout the late 1860s and the 1870s the threat of expensive sewerage schemes remained a constant worry to the suburban councils, particularly in poor Collingwood and Richmond, where it was complicated, as will be explained in chapters 6 and 7, by industrialization and the issue of Yarra pollution. We shall return to the topic of sewerage in chapter 8.

86

INDUSTRY, POLLUTION AND THE RIVER YARRA, 1850–65

6

Earlier chapters have shown that some suburbs became 'lower class' without passing through a preliminary stage of gentility. When and how, then, did inner suburbs become manufacturing areas?

Until 1851, when East Collingwood was still pastoral in appearance, it evidently had only two factories. Established in the late 1840s on allotments acquired from subdivider John Hodgson, they stood on the edge of the marshy Flat, virtually in the country. One factory, on two acres in Portion 55, was a coachbuilding and wheelwright works. For firewood, it first used trees cleared from the site. Equipped with steam power, it obtained contracts during the construction of the Studley Park bridge and the country railways in the late 1850s, and was still operating in 1888. The other factory, in Rokeby Street (Portion 54), was Victoria's first glass factory, but ceased to operate in the early 1850s. As explained later, the Glasshouse, as it was called, was subsequently a candle factory and then a tannery and boot factory.

Apart from these two isolated cases, industry in East Collingwood began in the 1850s. Victoria's soaring population increased meat consumption, which gave a boost to several trades associated with the processing of meat, fat, skin or hides. Thus East Collingwood gained the establishments for which it eventually became noted: fellmongeries, woolwasheries, tanneries, slaughterhouses, boiling-down works, piggeries and soap and candle works. Simultaneously, the population increase gave a boost to breweries and brickworks, and East Collingwood became a centre for these too.

Until about 1860, these establishments were tiny, providing relatively little employment for East Collingwood's booming population. Then, as explained later, a movement developed for the protection and expansion of industry in Collingwood in order to increase land values, to increase municipal revenue and to absorb the suburb's cheap labour. While industry grew, so did the problem of river and air pollution and so did Collingwood's reputation for filth, smells and miasma.

Fellmongers (sheepskin dealers), woolscourers (or woolwashers) and tanners became established in Richmond and East Collingwood, in that order, about the beginning of the 1850s. They were attracted there, rather than to residential areas like Fitzroy and Carlton, because of the Yarra as a free water supply for washing skins and wool and as a sewer and garbage dump.

At this time, Melbourne's only drinking water (apart from roof water) was obtained from the Yarra (via pumps and water carts). The Yarra was pure and clear at Collingwood, although it deteriorated lower down. In 1851 a Melbourne City Council special committee investigated Yarra pollution and counted four fellmongers and a tanner operating upstream at northern Richmond (then part of the municipality of Melbourne), near the Collingwood boundary. The committee recommended prohibiting new establishments, but in 1854 another special committee found they had increased to eight, handling a total of 5,000 sheepskins and 200 cattle hides a week, and had spread across the boundary into Collingwood outside the City Council's jurisdiction. The City Council feared that pollution from Collingwood and Richmond would increase, especially if a busy steamboat traffic stirred up submerged refuse. 'The poisonous gases evolved', said an engineer's opinion adopted by the council, 'will be found to have a most injurious effect upon the public health.'

Powerless to act outside its own boundary, the City Council prompted the introduction of a Yarra Pollution Prevention Bill into the Legislative Council in 1855. The Bill originally sought to prohibit all offensive factories above Melbourne, including the existing ones. The Legislative Council split into sides, led by two incompatible Collingwood residents—Francis Murphy (who lived on the Yarra, next to a fellmongery, and was anti-factory) and John Pascoe Fawkner (of Smith Street, who was pro-factory). The two sides wrangled over whether to pay compensation to the existing owners and how much. The manufacturers, in a petition, protested that they faced ruin if forced to leave. As a compromise, the eventual legislation tolerated the existing factories but prohibited their enlargement or the establishment of any more.

In 1855 Collingwood had six wool and skin establishments—in Portions 59, 60 and 63. Compared with the typical Collingwood shack having a net annual value of less than £25, the riverside factories had quite substantial buildings. For example, one of the proprietors of Portion 60 was Richard Goldsbrough, a pioneer in the Australian wool-dealing business, who had a large stone house there. The East Collingwood Council respected these gentlemen —and tolerated their operations—because they were an important source of rates.

The biggest of these factories was probably Peter Nettleton's in Portion 63. Nettleton had worked in the Yorkshire woollen cloth-making trade from the age of nine. Reaching Melbourne in 1849, aged twenty-five, he found employment at fellmongery and woolscouring, the nearest to his own trade. In 1852, after success-fully gold-digging, he bought into Portion 63, built a cottage, helped organize the construction of Simpson's Road (Victoria Street) and gradually flourished in fellmongering and woolscour-ing, with a considerable export trade.

During the 1860s, in contravention of the 1855 legislation, Col-lingwood's six fellmongeries and woolwasheries grew in size, and three tanneries were established. (These developments will be examined in detail in chapter 7.) Similar growth occurred in Richmond.

In 1870 one woolwashery alone (Nettleton's) cleaned 3,000 sheep-skins a week, and one tannery (in Richmond) tanned 300 cattle hides and 50 sheepskins a week. Several of the establishments said they engaged twenty-five to thirty (or even fifty) men daily. Some men—e.g., skilled tanners—were relatively well paid, but most jobs, especially in fellmongeries, were for unskilled labourers. These labourers, a local doctor observed, were 'mostly of dissipated habits —a class of unfortunate people who cannot get employment else-where'.[1]

The fellmongery and woolwashing process in Collingwood and Richmond was as follows. The sheepskins were collected from slaughteryards and were soaked in the Yarra for several days, gener-ally upon a pier-like timber framework encroaching perhaps half way across the river. Then they remained in a 'sweating-house' for several days until they decomposed sufficiently to allow the wool to be easily peeled off. Next the wool was scoured (i.e., soaked) in hot water with soap and soda, rinsed in the Yarra, dried and packed for export. Much solid refuse—pelts, heads and legs—had to be dis-posed of. Before 1870, it was dumped in the Yarra. After 1870, to satisfy public opinion, fellmongers claimed (unconvincingly) to have reformed. The heads and legs, they said, were now carted away; the pelts, if not required by tanners, were hung, still decomposing, to dry on rails in the open air and were exported to Britain, although this was not lucrative. Even so, the sheepskins that entered these establishments in 1870 were twice as heavy as the wool and refuse that was claimed to be carted away; that is, half the material that arrived went into the Yarra—an estimated 160 tons annually of animal and earthy matter (blood, grease, dirt and dung), and the suds from twenty tons of soap. As well as river pollution, there was air pollution for miles around ('a sickening odour'), caused by the peeling of wool from the skins, by the festering accumulation of offal, and by the absence of deodorization.

Tanneries were no less obnoxious than fellmongeries. At a typical tannery, sixty cattle hides (or perhaps a number of sheepskins) were soaked overnight in a pit of clean water, then for eight days in a pit containing lime water and, while the hair and flesh were being scraped off, the hides were soaked twice more. All this water (and also, until at least 1870, the hair) went into the Yarra. Next, to soften them, the hides were soaked for several days in a 'bate' of fowl or pigeon dung dissolved in water; this, too, went into the Yarra. At one tannery alone, one pit of bate was used a week, and three or four pits of lime. Finally, the hides were washed in clean water, and then remained in tan pits for several months according to the nature and the quality of the leather required in England (whether destined for making footwear, belting, harness, saddles, suitcases, gloves, upholstery, bookbinding, aprons or razor strops). The tanneries always resisted suggestions that they should install precipitating tanks and filters to limit Yarra pollution. A general feeling that no capital should be expended except on works which were wholly unavoidable seemed to pervade the trade.

Similar to the fellmongeries and tanneries were the soap and candle factories.

Collingwood's soap and candle industry became established in 1855, when Thomas Rae and associates enlarged William Overton's disused Glasshouse in Rokeby Street, Portion 54. Rae began making stearine candles which, he said, would be superior to, and cheaper than, the old offensive tallow candles that were made in England from Australian tallow and re-imported to Australia. Although the Glasshouse was formerly 'in the country', it was now surrounded by new cottages. The householders began complaining about air pollution from the boiling process. They had invested in the locality before Rae, they said, and their property had now been greatly depreciated overnight. The issue was raised against

Rae when in October 1856 he stood unsuccessfully for election to the East Collingwood Council. The council, then controlled by Rae's political enemies (Faction X) from the Johnston Street area, summoned representatives from the Central Board of Health who ordered Rae to abate the nuisance. About the end of the 1850s Rae retired and closed the candleworks.

A later, more successful soap and candle business was Henry Walker's on the Yarra. Walker had worked as a commercial traveller in England; he reached Melbourne in 1855 and worked as a book-keeper, salesman and manager for various businesses, including a small soap and candle factory in Victoria Street, Portion 63. In 1863, aged forty-two, he became owner of this business; by 1875 it was employing fifteen men and was producing fifty-five tons of soap and six tons of candles monthly.

In 1863 Walker acquired an additional property nearby—a 66 ft frontage in Portion 62—where he established a stearine candle factory. In the 1870s, because of price cutting by a rival manufacturer, he temporarily ceased operations at the stearine factory, converted it into a wax match factory, and added a shed where he smelted antimony. He later enlarged the stearine works. In 1868–88 Walker also owned a soap and candle factory at West Melbourne.

The making of soap and candles polluted both the Yarra and Collingwood's atmosphere. Butchers' fat was collected and sorted: the best grades were selected for fine candles and the lesser grades (perhaps including entrails with dung, thereby producing inferior tallow) for soap. The fat was boiled with water in vats. Before 1870 the vats were usually open, resulting in 'unbearable odours' even across the river in Hawthorn. In 1870 Henry Walker added carbolic acid to the melting fat as a deodorant (the less pure the fat, the more acid was needed), but the odours were still 'disgustingly offensive'. Walker claimed to have introduced air-tight vats, but still left tallow uncovered in the open air in order to bleach the tallow before making it into candles. The offensiveness of the whole process was increased if uncleaned entrails were used, and if there was any delay in putting them to boil. A final problem was in disposing of the residue of the boiling; Walker said that his went to market gardeners. The water used in washing the vats evidently went into the Yarra.

Closely associated with the fellmongeries, tanneries and soap and candle factories were the butchers and slaughtermen who supplied the skins and fat. Butchers and slaughtermen were a powerful lobby in Collingwood, favouring noxious trades and disregarding sanitary regulations.

In the 1850s, before public abattoirs had been established in Victorian cities and towns, butchers everywhere slaughtered at the rear of their shops. The first East Collingwood Council in 1855 institutionalized this practice by extracting a licence fee from the butchers. Property owners, both inside and outside the council, welcomed any such opportunity to boost the municipal revenue, as this helped to keep the general rate down to one shilling in the pound. The Central Board of Health complained about the butchers' premises: accumulations of blood and offal, sometimes oozing through rotten floorboards; pig-keeping; and overflowing cesspits. Neighbours complained about blood flowing down street channels from the Slope to the Flat, and about air pollution from the boiling-down of fat. For years the council did little more than issue warnings to the worst offenders.

In addition, the council in 1857 gladly began accepting fees from a large Fitzroy butcher, Charles Alexander, for the right to operate meatworks (comprising a slaughterhouse, a boiling-down plant and a piggery) in Clifton Hill, beside the Merri Creek. At first Alexander's works seemed rather remote from Collingwood's population. Smells from the works were dispersed by wind; the overflow of blood and offal gravitated to become diluted in the Yarra. The council was not concerned that the works were within a few hundred yards of the Yarra Bend Lunatic Asylum, Fairfield, and that the inmates were tormented by air pollution. The asylum superintendent complained bitterly to the council for years, but the lunatics were beyond the municipal boundary and beyond consideration. Alexander continued to enjoy the protection of East Collingwood councillors for the next thirty years. He also established slaughtering works at West Melbourne and a poultry farm at Preston.

In 1861 (the year Melbourne City Council opened public abattoirs at Flemington and prohibited backyard slaughtering in the City of Melbourne), East Collingwood Council decided to erect public abattoirs at Clifton Hill, not far from Alexander's meatworks. The government suggested that the East Collingwood abattoirs should be joint ones for several neighbouring municipalities but, as in the case of a joint mechanics' institute (see p. 69) and a joint manure depot (see p. 78), East Collingwood Council refused to allow any other council to exercise power within East Collingwood.

For the next twenty-four years the council let the abattoirs to one or two large butchers. These butchers, who were usually from Fitzroy, included Charles Alexander. These, in turn, charged fees for other butchers wishing to slaughter there. For a further fee, the council permitted butchers and other stockowners to graze their animals on newly acquired municipal reserves in Clifton Hill. These revenues were a further aid for a low general rate, at the cost of Collingwood's odious reputation.

Although backyard slaughtering now became illegal in both East Collingwood and Fitzroy, it remained common throughout the 1860s. For one reason, the new abattoirs were too small to accommodate the three dozen or more butchers of Fitzroy and East Collingwood. Secondly, the abattoirs were badly drained, and were mismanaged and uninviting; butchers worked knee-deep in accumulations of blood, offal, dung and mud. Thirdly, butchers considered the abattoirs an avoidable expense. To avoid paying fees to the lessees, some butchers slaughtered in a quarry just outside the abattoirs; to avoid paying road tolls and to save on transportation, most others still slaughtered at home. With such savings, an occasional fine was trifling.

In 1864, when fines increased, the butchers conducted a steady campaign to win toleration from councillors and honorary justices. The butchers included some resourceful and influential men. John Pritchard, a leader of the abattoirs boycott, had reached Victoria in 1852 aged twenty-one and, after goldfield experience, was one of the original traders in Smith Street; he eventually became one of the wealthiest, with a stylish residence at Clifton Hill.

Butchers joined with other shopkeepers in endorsing or opposing council candidates. For example, butcher William Tucker participated in a press advertisement supporting publican James Cattach and in another advertisement supporting baker Joseph Bowring; both candidates were elected and both, presumably, watched the interests of all traders, including Tucker. And a conscientious inspector of nuisances asked East Collingwood Council what to do with a £1 note sent to his wife by a butcher.

Finally, a friendly local bench acquitted one butcher because the council had failed to show that satisfactory facilities existed at the abattoirs. Henceforth butchers in both municipalities slaughtered as they liked with impunity. John Pritchard alone was killing fifty sheep a week away from the abattoirs.

While Fitzroy's twenty-two butchers were complaining about insufficient accommodation at East Collingwood abattoirs, Fitzroy

Council considered erecting abattoirs of its own in North Fitzroy, but residents there objected. Eventually East Collingwood and Fitzroy agreed that the former would extend its abattoirs, while the latter would erect none. Thus East Collingwood would benefit financially, at the cost of confirming its bad reputation, while Fitzroy would be rid of a nuisance—another component in the sanitary difference between the two municipalities.

Despite the enlarged abattoirs, butchers in both municipalities continued their boycott, still complaining about insufficient accommodation, although the main reason was still probably expense. Fitzroy Council lost patience with the butchers and resumed fining them, without much success.

In the 1870s, the largest Fitzroy and Collingwood butchers began killing in the country, near Preston. By then, the Collingwood abattoirs, filthier than ever, were being used largely by butchers from outside the district. Collingwood Council, still making money from the abattoirs (£300 a year) as well as from Charles Alexander's meatworks, delayed closing the abattoirs and meatworks until the decision became unavoidable during epidemic scares in the 1880s. Cases of boiling-down or slaughtering at Collingwood and Fitzroy butchers' shops persisted into the 1890s.

Brewing was one of Collingwood's first and fastest-growing industries. By 1863 there were six breweries and two distilleries. These make an interesting case study in the suburb's industrialization. At first, until the 1860s, the entrepreneurs lived locally, made their own liquor and were personally known to the drinkers. In seeking to extend the scope of their industry, they became involved with councillors and parliamentarians. Gradually, in the 1860s and 1870s, they increased their premises, staff, output and fortunes, while the business became more mechanized and more metropolitan in scope. Finally, in the 1880s, the family firms passed into the hands of city-based companies whose directors lived in better suburbs.

In the early 1850s two breweries were established on the Yarra—George Coppin's in Portion 63 and Thomas Graham's in Portion 62. One of these was described thus in an auction advertisement: half an acre fronting the river; a brick brew-house (suitable, alternatively, as a distillery) measuring 20 ft by 15 ft by 30 ft, with a large wooden tank of 1,800 gallons capacity, and a corrugated iron store measuring 18 ft by 30 ft, a six-horsepower steam engine, two steam boilers and a Yarra-water pump. Coppin's brewery was defunct by the early 1860s. Graham's brewery was later re-named the Shamrock Brewery and considerably developed.

The third brewery in the Collingwood district was Thomas Aitken's Victoria Brewery, which still stands in Victoria Parade, East Melbourne, on the Melbourne side of the Melbourne-Collingwood boundary. Aitken arrived in Melbourne in 1842 and commenced a brewery in Geelong in 1851. He established the Victoria Brewery in 1854 when he was aged thirty-one, and steadily enlarged it until in the 1870s it had a seven-storey brewing tower, 87 ft high, with a hydraulic lift. The Victoria Brewery's employees increased from 13 in 1854 to 31 in 1862, 40 in 1883 and 80 in 1888. In 1862 the brewery kept sixteen horses for transport and hundreds of cats (including wild ones in the cellar) to catch rats.

By 1860 Aitken was an influential figure in the embryonic Protectionist movement and, as we shall see later in this chapter, was dealing with members of parliament and municipal councillors. In 1862 Aitken began operating a distillery in Northumberland Street, East Collingwood (Portion 53)—claimed to be the first distillery established after the imposition of the differential duty under the Distillation Act of 1861. In 1864 the distillery employed five or six hands; its carting was done by the Victoria Brewery.

Collingwood's fourth brewery began in Bedford Street (Portion 73) in the mid-1850s. About 1860 it was purchased by Edward Wild in association with Charles Vaughan, M.L.C., later chairman of Fitzroy Council. Wild, an active Protectionist, enthusiastically promoted 'colonial ales' in competition with imported ales.

Collingwood's fifth brewer was John Wood, who arrived in 1848, aged twenty-two. He operated first as a building contractor and settled in Wellington Street, East Collingwood (Portion 53), where in the late 1850s he successively opened three businesses—a wine and spirit store, the Yorkshire Arms Hotel and the Yorkshire Brewery. By 1864, judging from that year's ratebook, he was already one of the largest owners of East Collingwood property. Initially, Wood brewed in a wooden building, using a 36-gallon copper. In 1877, with sons as partners, he built a six-storey brewing tower, with a hydraulic lift, a 205 ft high chimney stack and stabling for twenty-six horses.

With their multi-storey brewing towers topped by a spire and flag-pole, Aitken and Wood certainly left their mark upon Collingwood. Together with two shot towers built in Collingwood about the same time, these breweries were the district's tallest buildings,

Yorkshire Brewery, Wellington Street, Collingwood, 1890.

rivalling the churches of other suburbs and symbolizing the future Collingwood.

In contrast with the heights of Aitken and Wood, Collingwood's sixth brewery (Crisp's Burton Brewery in Cambridge Street, Portion 53) was noted for its low chimney and for its air pollution.

Collingwood's second distillery was opened in Sackville Street (Portion 81) about 1863 by Thomas Miles, a former contractor. Miles recalled that during 1852–3 he had been employing 'hundreds of men all round Melbourne in making streets'. Entering East Collingwood Council in 1864, he was immediately elected mayor, but before his term of office expired he had become bankrupt, and the distillery had several subsequent owners. In 1883 the distillery had half a dozen employees.

Breweries were conducted with some offence, although not as much as other noxious trades. Apart from air pollution, the main complaint concerned refuse water from the washing of casks, which (at the riverside breweries) drained directly into the Yarra or (in most cases) oozed across the street channels of the Flat.

The subsequent development of breweries is described in chapter 9.

Brickmaking began in East Collingwood in the late 1850s, in Portions 61 and 62 beside the Yarra.

According to Titles Office records, Portion 62 had remained in the hands of the original Crown grantee (J. T. E. Flint, shipowner, of London) until he subdivided it into large pieces in 1853. In 1858 eight brickmakers there claimed to have about £15,000 invested in their business. They asked the council to form and metal Brick Lane (later re-named Flockhart Street) and offered to contribute £40.

Portion 61, originally granted to Captain William Lonsdale, administrator of Port Phillip, passed through a complicated sequence of mortgages during the 1840s. The portion was subdivided by estate agents in 1858. Some of the allotments were purchased by Dr William Crooke, who leased them to brickmakers.

Crooke arrived in 1857 from Tasmania, where he had been a surgeon, pastoralist and member of parliament. He also bought allotments in other parts of Collingwood and in other suburbs. He developed a large medical practice on the Hill in Fitzroy, safe from his kiln fumes, and became a key figure in Victoria's Protectionist movement, helping to place Protectionists in parliament and in municipal councils.

The mid-1860s saw the beginnings of the boot-manufacturing industry, for which Collingwood later became noted. This was a logical development of several conditions existing in Collingwood: the supply of leather, the concentration of shoemakers and the supply of cheap labour.

One firm in Wellington Street began making boot uppers. The leather was received from a tanner, and after undergoing a process of blocking and being stitched by machine or hand, was supplied to Collingwood's many freelance bootmakers. The Collingwood products were said to be better than imports, because the latter, packed closely in cases, had 'steamed and sweated during the long voyage'.

Further advanced along the scale of industrialization was the Collingwood Tannery and Boot Factory Limited, which began in 1864 in the Glasshouse building in Portion 54. The six foundation shareholders were city men, except for Councillor Thomas Greenwood, who was a minor shareholder with ten £5 shares. Using steam, the factory began with about twenty men and boys; later in the 1860s, aided by a tariff, the employees increased to 200, with wages totalling £300 a week. The company made its own leather in its tannery of thirty-six tanpits; this section employed twenty men. The company produced 75,000 pairs of boots, shoes and slippers a year, exporting some to other colonies.

Thus, significantly, the tanning industry had spread from the sparsely populated riverside towards the densely populated Slope, half a mile from the Yarra. Effluent from the Glasshouse tanpits entered the earth channels of Rokeby Street, and oozed slowly across the Flat, past the windows of workers' cottages, towards the Yarra—an obvious breach of the Yarra pollution legislation.

For about twenty years from 1869 the factory was controlled by Hugh Thomson, a city leather merchant who lived in pleasant East Melbourne.

Having surveyed Collingwood's early industries, we shall now examine moves that were made to accelerate their development.

From about 1859 onwards, the story of Collingwood's industrial development becomes linked with the growing demand in Victoria for discriminative duties to be imposed on imported goods in order to foster employment among Victoria's skilled trades. Other writers have shown how Protection was advocated from the early 1850s at Geelong (first by the *Geelong Advertiser* and later by Geelong district farmers), how similar agitation developed early in 1859 among the industrial population of the metropolis, and how Protection evolved from a secondary issue at the 1859 parliamentary elections (after land reform) to a major issue at the elections of 1861, 1864 and 1865, gradually absorbing the impetus of the older land reform movement.[2] What needs stressing here is that Collingwood was one of the suburbs where the demand for Protection first became noticeable and where it received perhaps its greatest support. The struggle between Protection and Free Trades in the metropolis is largely a struggle between Protectionist industrial suburbs on the one hand and the City of Melbourne (the centre of commercial and Free Trade interests) on the other. As the subsequent development of Victoria's Protection movement as a whole is well known, the following pages will concentrate on this suburban aspect.

In 1859, when Collingwood's population was rising without a commensurate increase in employment opportunities, Collingwood men were conspicuous in the newly established Tariff Reform League of Victoria. The league held public meetings in the city and suburbs, including Collingwood, questioned parliamentary candidates, urged electors to support certain candidates and petitioned parliament for a review of the fiscal system. The only outcome at this stage was Collingwood parliamentarian Thomas Embling's Select Committee upon the Tariff, which recommended a tariff revision. Among the witnesses were Collingwood men who related how conditions had deteriorated in skilled trades during the later 1850s and how, because of cheap imported goods, thousands of craftsmen around Melbourne including skilled bootmakers, saddlers, carpenters and cabinet makers, were unable to find work in their own trades.

Two of these witnesses were saddlemaker William Prytherch (a Welsh surname, pronounced *Prith*-rick) and bootmaker Henry Turnbull, both of Wellington Street (Portion 53). They said that in 1859 they were each employing one or two men or boys—fewer than when they had arrived in Victoria before the gold rush—and that much of their business in 1859 was in selling imported goods. As property-owners, these witnesses were rather small men. According to our search of the 1864 ratebook, Turnbull and Prytherch each owned Collingwood property amounting to only £66 net annual value. But they were competent political agitators, and they both became key figures in the Victorian Protectionist movement.

Turnbull had an interesting background. Scottish born, he arrived in Sydney in 1838 and became noted for his participation in anti-transportation agitation there and also later in Melbourne. He was active in the East Collingwood Local Committee (see p. 38) from 1853 to 1855 and was a member of Faction Q in the council (see p. 59) in the 1860s.

A detailed study of a suburb such as Collingwood can contribute to our understanding of Victorian Protectionism in general. For example, the minute books of the East Collingwood Council from October 1855 to January 1863 give the names of all candidates at the thirteen council elections (by-elections as well as general ones) and also give the names of the men who proposed and seconded them at the public nomination meetings—information which often cannot be found in newspapers. An analysis of the 80 nominations and 160 endorsements reveals that men who were to be prominent Protectionists in the 1860s began to significantly influence the composition of the council in October 1859 and that they dominated it after October 1860. Thus it emerges that Protectionists sought to capture not only the central government (as is well known) but also local government, and that they succeeded in at least one local government before they did in the central one.

Furthermore, from the nominations and endorsements, it is possible to discern patterns of association among councillors and also between councillors and their lay supporters. In the five years beginning in October 1860 the council usually included a Protectionist brewer (first Thomas Aitken, then Edward Wild, then Thomas Miles). Closely associated with these were other active Protectionists—e.g., bootmaker Turnbull, saddlemaker Prytherch, house-painter George Payne, tanner Robert Flockhart, woolwasher Isaac Reeves, brickmaker William Crooke and Charles Jardine Don, M.L.A. These men repeatedly nominated one another for council. According to the minute books for 1860–3, Thomas Aitken, for example, was nominated by William Crooke and William Prytherch; Isaac Reeves was nominated by William Crooke (twice) and others; Robert Flockhart was nominated by Charles Don and William Prytherch; Edward Wild was nominated by William Crooke and bootmaker Thomas Heales; and so on. Other councillors associating with this circle included three publicans (John Wood, Thomas Greenwood and Peter Petherick) and two shopkeepers (James Houghton and Benjamin Clark). This chain of relationships is illustrated by the case of Benjamin Clark, a Scottish former bootmaker who (presumably through economic necessity) had become a boot importer and dealer. In 1860–3 Clark nominated six candidates including Don, Payne, Turnbull and public servant John Noone; in 1867 he entered the council himself. At the council table, unless other personal factors (e.g., geographical rivalry) intervened, all the men mentioned above tended to vote for each other's motions on matters concerning East Collingwood's general economic development.

To see the complexity of Protectionists' motives and relationships, let us consider Charles Jardine Don, who became famous as one of the first working-class parliamentarians anywhere in the British Empire to identify himself with that class. As Don's many achievements and admirable personal qualities are recorded in the *Australian Dictionary of Biography*, we shall concentrate here on forgotten aspects of his circumstances. Don, a stonemason, was active in Chartist and other radical movements in Scotland in the 1840s and in movements for land reform and for an eight-hours day in Victoria in the 1850s. A powerful and useful orator, he was welcomed in Collingwood radical circles in 1859 and, although hitherto a rabid Freetrader, was requisitioned to contest the Collingwood electorate. According to old associates later, he reluctantly converted to Protection during the election but remained a Freetrader at heart. Don topped the poll in the three-member constituency, repeating this feat in 1861.

Since there were no salaries for parliamentarians, Don was plagued by the problem of earning a living. He continued for a short while as a stonemason, but was inconvenienced by late-night sittings and wanted to attend day-time committee meetings. In February 1860, at a hotel on Collingwood Flat, he was entertained at a public function attended by two hundred people, and was given a testimonial of £200. Soon he dropped his trade and relied increasingly on the favours of supporters. While in parliament, his health was failing and he drank heavily.

In October 1860 Don gained election to East Collingwood Council, along with brewer Thomas Aitken (a fellow Scot) and a third candidate. Although not a property-owner, Don was eligible for election since he was liable to pay rates for a house he was renting in Elizabeth Street (Portion 53). As explained in chapter 4, a group of ratepayers interested in Elizabeth Street (whom we called Faction Q) were about to persuade the council to transform Elizabeth Street into a busy, valuable thoroughfare (later called Langridge Street). These ratepayers (led by Henry Turnbull, in association with Thomas Greenwood, John Newlands, John Noone, George Payne and James Houghton) were all Protectionists. Faction Q's aim in transforming Elizabeth Street was to increase land values there and also to 'protect' and foster Collingwood's native industry. 'Industry' meant not only Turnbull's bootmaking, Prytherch's saddlemaking, Aitken's brewing and distilling (he was about to establish his Northumberland Street distillery), but also the business of countless shopkeepers, publicans, contractors and landlords. It is not necessary to regard these men as merely self-seeking; they believed that what was good for business was good for Collingwood. Thus Councillor Don made the improvement of Elizabeth Street one of his chief concerns. Together with Greenwood, Aitken, Houghton and another councillor, he was a member of the council's improvement committee, which drafted the controversial East Collingwood Improvement Bill (see pp. 59–60). He introduced the Bill to parliament, and lobbied for its support. It is not known now who was Don's landlord in Elizabeth Street, or what was the amount of the rent, but it is highly likely that the landlord was Henry Turnbull (a fellow Scot) and that the house was rent-free. In April 1861 Don and Aitken simultaneously resigned from the council, together with another councillor. These vacancies were filled by three of the Faction Q Protectionists—Turnbull, Payne and Noone. In August 1861 a well-organized campaign returned Don (and the Protectionist Heales government) to parliament. Clearly Don was playing one role in an extensive operation, involving master tacticians.

A further inkling of pressures facing impecunious parliamentarians in the 1860s is given in an editorial in the Collingwood *Observer* in 1909. Before the introduction of parliamentary salaries, the editorial says, such parliamentarians were 'placed in a contemptible position'.

> They had to live on bribes—no measure could be got through without bribing members—or become slaves of a faction. Thus the Heales Government [of 1861] subsidised out of the ministerial salaries six men required to give the balance of power. These pensioners had their board paid [at two hotels].[3]

The editorial does not name the six members, but goes on: 'The first Labor member, Don, obtained, in the name of his partner, a number of small government contracts untendered for.' This evidently refers to a building partnership which Don had with a fellow Scottish stonemason, William Smith of East Collingwood. Unfortunately the editorial does not elaborate or substantiate these allegations, but it provides a lead for possible future research.

In 1861 associates established Don as a tobacconist in Bourke

Street near Parliament House, apparently without success. In January 1862, through Aitken, Don began renting, and obtained a licence for, the Rifle Brigade Hotel, Brunswick Street, Fitzroy. Don had signed a deed of indenture with Aitken, but it is not known what rent he paid, if any. Aitken owned the freehold of several hotels, and was thus anticipating the practice, common in the twentieth century, of breweries owning hotels and installing celebrities in them as licensees. His hotels were available as venues for Protection meetings. After a year Don parted from the Rifle Brigade, and his occupation was being given simply as 'Member of the Legislative Assembly'.

In 1861 Don offended his supporters by approving of the Duffy land Bill. Although Don finally voted against it, he gradually lost electoral support and was unseated in 1864. Before the 1864 election he stressed (apparently with regret) that there was no official reward for his hard work, although, he said, public servants and parliamentary lawyers were well rewarded. He said that he had been offered bribes to vote in the interests of squatters but had refused.[4]

Before dying from pulmonary consumption in 1866, Don lost money in speculations and had to rely on financial assistance from friends. Among the many donors was Ambrose Kyte, M.L.A., who had access to ample funds and who was generous in subsidizing needy politicians.

An *Observer* memoir of the 1890s, referring back to about 1870, recalls that Thomas Aitken, together with Smith Street draper Mark Foy, used to 'run' a candidate for the Collingwood parliamentary seat. The article claims that in the 1870s 'no man need expect to be elected for Collingwood unless he was under the thumb of the draper and brewer alluded to'.[5] This article refers to a period after Don's death, but it whets one's appetite for more information about Aitken's dealings before then.

Collingwood remained at the forefront of Victoria's Protectionist movement during the political crises of 1863–5. A Labour, Protection and Tariff Reform League was formed in East Collingwood and Fitzroy in 1863, with a committee comprising three shoemakers, two carpenters, two house-painters (George Payne and his brother), a saddler (Prytherch), a cabinetmaker and a piano manufacturer. Supported by Graham Berry's *Observer*, the Collingwood league held large public meetings—first at the Studley Arms Hotel, then in other suburbs and next (after Melbourne interests had denounced the movement as a mere Collingwood agitation) at Ballarat and in the City of Melbourne. Of the five candidates for the Collingwood electorate in 1864, four were Protectionists; of the three elected, two were Protectionists.

Not all tradesmen were Protectionists, however. John Myers, a former London bootmaker who supported Chartism in the 1840s and almost every radical movement in Victoria in the 1850s, remained a staunch Freetrader all his life. At an East Collingwood public meeting in 1865, he attacked Protection because it would benefit seventeen trades but not fifty-four others. The meeting refused to hear him.

In Collingwood-Fitzroy the Free Trade movement was identified chiefly with City of Melbourne importers. The few local bulwarks of Free Trade were retailers: William and Thomas Kidney (big Smith Street importers, outfitters and shoe merchants), J. W. Randell (Smith Street haberdasher), and Edward Langton, M.L.A. (a Fitzroy butcher who became secretary of the Free Trade League). The *Observer* commented: 'Mr. Langton was sent over the country as a soft goods evangel to organise a Free Trade League ... The fact that the Chamber of Commerce, plus a few Randells and Kidneys, constituted the Free Trade League was carefully suppressed [in England].'[6]

In the early 1860s, as the development of Collingwood lagged behind that of inland towns such as Ballarat, it seemed that the rapid development of a staple industry was needed to save Collingwood. Some people, naturally, longed for a Collingwood gold rush. After a gold speck was reported at Studley Park in 1862, a Collingwood Gold Mining Company was floated and a shaft was sunk through bluestone to 100 ft in Hoddle Street at the corner of Gipps Street. After slow progress because of financial difficulties, the mine revived in 1865 by suddenly 'producing' a pennyworth of gold. Graham Berry was appointed manager, but the company finally lapsed in 1866. The Collingwood gold mine showed how industry could improve the Flat. During the sensation of 1865, crowds flocked to the mine. Councillor John Anderson's nearby Royal George Hotel did a roaring trade. Thomas Grimwood, who operated the rival Victoria Hotel further up Hoddle Street, even tried to establish a mine near his own hotel.

Industrialization became central to ideas about environmental improvement. As stated in chapter 4, the council's plans for drainage in 1865 were designed partly to encourage factories and partly to remove the factories' ill effects. This is reflected in a typical com-

ment by the *Observer*: 'As an earnest of their [the councillors']
friendly intentions towards those gentlemen who invest capital in
the locality, it was agreed to kerb and channel Bedford Street,
adjoining the brewery of Mr. E. Wild.' Looking forward to a new
East Collingwood with factories and metalled thoroughfares (in
contrast to its muddy, humble beginnings), the *Observer* said:

> Apart from its gold-field, East Collingwood possesses many of the
> elements of prosperity, and may yet become the Manchester of the
> Southern Hemisphere . . . Being one of the most densely populated
> suburbs . . . there is always an abundant supply—too much, unfortu-
> nately, of late years—of labour, which only requires the application of
> capital to be utilised. Already several industries have been successfully
> launched, and there is talk of others being initiated as soon as some
> protection from foreign competition can be guaranteed.[7]

This theme was still current a decade later when a council candidate—Robert Dehnert, brickmaker, of Portion 62—declared that he
wanted 'as many factories on the Yarra as possible; this would be
the only way to make Collingwood a second Manchester, as the
district was naturally formed for industrial establishments'.[8]

The contrast which we have been sketching—between, on one
hand, advocates of industrialization in Collingwood and, on the
other, non-industrial interests centred largely in the City of Melbourne—illuminates a controversy (discussed in the next chapter)
about the use of the River Yarra. Was the Yarra provided by a
benevolent Nature (as industrialist Dehnert implied) primarily as
a sewer for Collingwood industrialists? Or was the Yarra valuable
(as non-industrialists downstream believed) for other reasons?

THE DEATH OF THE RIVER YARRA
1860–80

7

We have seen, in the previous chapter, how Collingwood's industry began in a small way in the 1850s, largely along the Yarra, and how ambitious persons in the early 1860s regarded Collingwood as ideal for capital investment. The main obstacle to this goal was the legislation of 1855 which prohibited the enlargement of Yarra-polluting factories or the establishment of any more. The present chapter concerns attempts to overcome this obstacle.

The growing interest in industrialization in East Collingwood in the 1860s is reflected in the occupations of councillors. One useful way of measuring occupational trends in the council is to divide councillors (rather arbitrarily) into two categories as shown in Table 7—'non-industrial' (men with a stake in a shop or a piece of land or a profession) and 'industrial' (concerned with the production of goods). Our table shows that, for the first five years (1855–9), the council was almost wholly 'non-industrial'. A typical combination would be four proprietors of local retailing establishments (including a grocer, a baker and a publican), two local landowners and a Melbourne businessman. 'Industrial' occupations hardly appeared until 1860, and they remained in a minority for another half decade (with the exception of one year, 1861), but thereafter (from August 1867) 'industrial' always predominated over 'non-industrial' by at least five to four. (In 1864 the council was enlarged from seven to nine members.) A typical combination in the late 1860s would be three local retailers, two building contractors, a sawmiller and three proprietors of noxious trades.[1]

In practice the council was oriented towards industry, particularly towards riverside noxious trades, to an even greater extent than our table suggests. Any council candidate, whatever his occupation, was likely to be favourably disposed towards the noxious trades, since these were Collingwood's staple industries. For example, a building contractor was publicly endorsed as a candi-

106

TABLE 7

Occupations of Collingwood councillors, 1855–81, showing a tendency towards 'industrial' categories

| | 'Non-industrial' occupations | | | | | 'Industrial' occupations | | | | | |
| | Miscellaneous | | Local commercial | | | Non-noxious trades | | Noxious trades | | | |
Year	Gentlemen and professional	City commercial	Shop-keepers	Bakers	Publicans	Building contractors	Other artisans*	Tanners etc.†	Brewers	Soap makers	Brick-makers
1855	3	1	2		1						
1856	2	1	2		1	1					
1857	2	1	1	1	2						
1858	2		1	2	2	1					
1859		1	2	2	1	1					
1860		2	2		1	1					
1861		1	1		1		2	2	1		
1862		1	1		2			2	1		
1863		2			3		1	1	1		
1864		1		2	3	1		1			
1865		2		1	3	2	1				
1866		2		1	2	2	2				
1867			1	1	1	1	2	2			
1868	1		1	1	1	1	2	2			
1869			1		1	2	1	2			1
1870		1	1		1	2	1	2			1
1871		1	1		1	2	1	2			1
1872			2	1	1	2		2		1	1
1873	1		1	1	1	3	1	1		1	
1874	1		1		1	3	1			1	1
1875	1		2		1	2	1			1	1
1876	1		1		1	2	1			1	1
1877	1	1		1	1	2	1	1		1	1
1878	1	1		1	1	2	1	1		1	1
1879	2	1				2	2	1		1	
1880	2	1				2	2	1		1	
1881	1	1	1		1	2	2	1			

* Bootmakers, sawmillers, saddlers, coopers, painters.
† Including fellmongers and woolwashers.

date in 1866 by woolwashers Peter Nettleton and Isaac Reeves and by brickmaker Robert Dehnert. Like Thomas Aitken (chapter 6), Peter Nettleton was considered 'quite a Warwick' in parliamentary and municipal affairs. 'Whenever anyone aspired to political, municipal or School Board honours', the *Observer* recalled later, 'it was Peter Nettleton whose support they first sought. He was a tower of strength to those he backed, and he invariably backed his support with the needful when necessary.'

In contravention of the 1855 legislation, riverside factories in Collingwood and Richmond grew in size and number after 1859. The government and the City Council preferred noxious trades to be concentrated below Melbourne, around swampy Fishermen's Bend, towards the mouth of the Yarra, but entrepreneurs saw several advantages in Collingwood-Richmond. Firstly, the water upstream, being pure, not salty, was better for washing wool. Secondly, proprietors and employees could live comfortably near the works, whereas Fishermen's Bend was desolate; this factor was even more important in the 1860s, when the expanding factories were able to draw on Collingwood's pool of cheap labour. Thirdly, compared with Melbourne City Council, which controlled Fishermen's Bend, East Collingwood and Richmond Councils were much more tolerant.

Two incidents in 1860 illustrate this toleration. In February, residents of Portion 60 complained that Frederick Row's fellmongery was being extended. East Collingwood's part-time inspector of nuisances, Police Sergeant James Nimon, prosecuted Row, but the local bench, comprising honorary justices, dismissed the case because the extension 'did not proceed beyond the boundaries [i.e. the fences] of the property'. In May, James B. Hayman, who had just established a tannery in newly subdivided Portion 61, complained to the council that Sergeant Nimon had twice prosecuted him for infringing the pollution act. The council resolved that Hayman was blameless; it asked the local bench to dismiss the case so as to avoid 'increased expense to Mr Hayman', and dismissed Nimon as inspector. The council and the local bench were both recruited from the same pool of local businessmen, some of whom served in both capacities.

In 1860 East Collingwood Council, in consultation with Richmond Council, resolved to seek the repeal of the 1855 legislation so that the river could be 'thrown open to manufacturing enterprise'. The council convened public meetings, and set up a council committee (comprising five Protectionists, including a fellmonger and a tanner) to petition parliament through Charles Don, M.L.A.

It became fashionable for East Collingwood councillors or council candidates to publicly advocate repeal of the Yarra pollution laws. One said that the establishment of factories on the Yarra would be 'beneficial to the public interests, and, under proper supervision, less calculated to pollute the river than the present drainage system'. Another referred to 'abolishing the Yarra Protection Bill so as to facilitate the establishment of manufactories', and said that he would advocate 'anything that would induce capitalists to spend their money in East Collingwood'.

Accordingly, Collingwood and Richmond members of the Legislative Assembly made concerted assaults on the Yarra pollution laws in 1862, 1865, 1866 and 1867.[2] The Collingwood members concerned were John Edwards, Graham Berry and Charles Don in 1862; Edwards, Berry and George Harker in 1865; and Edwards, Thomas Embling and Isaac Reeves in 1866–7. Harker was the only Freetrader. Their chief collaborator from Richmond was J. G. Francis.

In 1862 the pro-industrialist members from Collingwood and Richmond sought to repeal the 1855 legislation. They appealed for support from 'all the Protectionists in the House', but failed to gain a majority of the House. The 'purificationists' (as we shall call those who wished to preserve the pollution legislation) included Ambrose Kyte who, although not a member for Collingwood, was chairman of the Collingwood Gas Company. East Collingwood Council later retaliated against Kyte by threatening to prosecute the Gas Company under the Yarra pollution laws for discharging offensive matter into the Yarra, via the Reilly Street open drain.

In 1865, while the government was consolidating all existing health laws, the pro-industrialists managed by a small majority (22 to 19) to strike out the Yarra pollution clauses, but three weeks later the clauses were re-inserted by a vote of 25 to 20 and three months after that the Assembly refused to reconsider the matter.

In 1866 while parliament was considering amendments to the public health laws, the pro-industrialists again managed to strike out the Yarra pollution clauses with significant majorities (23 votes to 12 on one day, 26 to 18 on another). The clauses were re-inserted by the Legislative Council, but the Assembly by a vote of 22 to 20 dissented from the Council and, because of this split between the houses, the health Bill perished that year. The purificationists of 1866 included Edward Langton, the Fitzroy butcher who was now secretary of the Free Trade League and member for East Melbourne. Like Ambrose Kyte, Langton was himself involved in the polluting of the Yarra; he had formerly conducted a private slaughterhouse on the Merri Creek at Clifton Hill.

In 1867, following an agreement between the government and the pro-industrialists, the health Bill was re-introduced without Yarra pollution clauses and was passed; the pro-industrialists moved to repeal the existing Yarra pollution laws by means of a separate Bill, but this, however, lapsed.

Technically, then, the pollution laws of 1855 and 1865 remained in force but, because of the confusion of 1865–7, their public standing was diminished.

Parliamentarians generally viewed the struggle in the context of wider tensions between sectional and general interests. In the 1862 debate, the tone was set in a clash between Peter Snodgrass (who was later found to have been involved in bribery and corruption of parliamentarians on behalf of squatters) and William McLellan (of the goldfields electorate of Ararat), as reported in *Hansard*:

> Mr. Snodgrass remarked that . . . in attempting to forward the interests of a certain number of people, [the pro-industrialists were] damaging the interests of the rest of the community. Speaking as a landowner on the Yarra, he believed that the effect of the passing of the repeal bill would be to reduce the value of the land on the river to a mere song.
>
> Mr. McLellan, seeing the quarter from whence the opposition to the bill proceeded, could almost suppose that the squatters, in addition to possessing the whole of the lands of the country, wished also to monopolise the whole of its waters. (Laughter) . . . Gentlemen who had built expensive residences on the Yarra were afraid that manufactories would spring up, and damage their property; but so far from the value of the property on the river being depreciated . . . it would be increased ten-fold; and he (Mr McLellan) knew individuals who would be too glad to give five times the present price for plots of land on the river if they were allowed to establish manufactories there.

Similarly W. M. K. Vale (West Ballarat) observed in 1866:

> The real question was, whether the banks of the Yarra should be conserved for the residences of a few wealthy men, or whether they should afford the means of employment for the large population that had settled at Collingwood and Richmond. It was a battle between the possessors of 500 villa residences and a population of 15,000 or 20,000.

The case for unlocking the Yarra, as presented in parliament, may be summarized as follows. The gold boom was over, and if capitalists could not invest in factories, they would be driven elsewhere. Many English towns had been made prosperous by manufacturing, and only manufacturing could make Melbourne what it ought to be. The existing Yarra factories in Richmond-Collingwood were employing hundreds of men, and were turning over £500,000 to £1,000,000 annually; this could be increased. The Yarra was the ideal stream for manufacturing. Unlike the Salt-water (Maribyrnong) River west of Melbourne, the Yarra was not salty, and Collingwood and Richmond already had a labour force. For about £3,000 a tunnel could be cut through Studley Park, shortening the horseshoe bend and (with a fall of about 9 ft) providing a stream of water sufficient to drive any amount of machinery. Unlike 1855, Melbourne's drinking water now came from the Yan Yean reservoir. In case the Yan Yean failed, large suburban reservoirs could be built, or Yarra water could be pumped from above Collingwood. Certainly, much offensive matter at present entered the river at Collingwood, but it came from street drains rather than from factories. And as the Yarra was already being polluted by drains, the establishment of manufactories would add little or no injury to this. Any filth would be speedily carried to the sea—especially if, as planned, the falls near Queen's Wharf in the city were removed. As for air pollution, tanneries had a wholesome influence on the air; one tanning district in England had escaped a cholera epidemic.

These arguments emerged from speaker after speaker, with variations according to personality. Thomas Embling, M.L.A. (a medical practitioner), was aggressively utilitarian. The Yarra, he said, was 'well adapted' for manufacturing and was 'required' for it. The 'useful arts' must take priority over leisure and luxury. The country 'could not afford' to keep the Yarra clean.

Isaac Godfrey Reeves, M.L.A., who operated a woolwashing establishment in Portion 59, expressed indignation and frustration. The locking of the Yarra, he said, was 'a heavy blow' aimed at the industrial classes.

> One gentleman, who had sunk £20,000 in endeavouring to establish an industry that would be of the greatest possible advantage to the country, and would consume a large portion of the raw material now sent home, would have to close his manufactory and endure the loss of his capital.

With an unlocked Yarra, the wages paid to the working classes there would quickly increase from the present £500 a week to £5,000. Unlocking the Yarra, he said, was even more important than Protection. He would prefer an unlocked Yarra to 'the largest measure of Protection that could be given the colony for the next ten years'. (Reeves later suffered business failures. He died in 1886 in seclusion.)

The 'purificationist' case in parliament may be summarized as follows. Yarra pollution might suit the people of Richmond and Collingwood but not the people of Melbourne downstream. The interests of Melbourne's 100,000 inhabitants were more important than the interests of a small handful of manufacturers. It appeared that, because East Collingwood was polluted, the whole course of the Yarra should be polluted. The Saltwater River was better for factories; reticulated pure water could be laid on there, and the river would be navigable to their very doors. The existing legislation was aimed against factories that polluted rather than against any other potential riverside factories; the river needed to be purified even if only to ensure a clean water supply for the latter category. In England, cholera and typhoid outbreaks had followed the course of smelly streams, and London was now incurring great expense in cleaning up the Thames. Man lived not by bread alone; a clean Yarra was needed for swimming, boating and fishing. (But, countered the pro-industrialists, fish were fated to vanish through the growth of steamboat traffic.) Anyway, said the purificationists, Melbourne ought to have underground sewerage.

Yarra pollution—and its relevance to Protection and land settlement—provoked eloquent editorials. The Collingwood *Observer* in 1865 campaigned for 'unlocking the Yarra for the people's factories' in much the same way as it campaigned for unlocking the land for agriculture, and identified the 'purificationist' cause with south-of-the-Yarra aristocrats. The Melbourne *Age* took a different line: it supported the establishment of factories, but not on the Yarra. The *Age* said that it wanted a pure Yarra not from the viewpoint of the southside elite but because of the interests of the Collingwood-Richmond working classes. The Collingwood-Richmond population

> would breathe the deadly miasma which would be given off by this sinuous stream. They would see their children struck down by febrile diseases, and would feel their own constitutions insidiously undermined by sleeping in an atmosphere laden with the elements of infection . . . People of the most robust systems are lowered in tone,

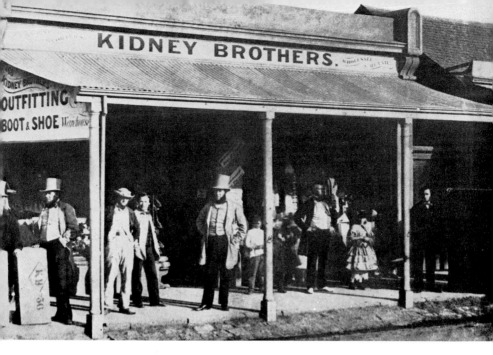

The principal store in Smith Street, Collingwood, about 1861.

The Earl of Zetland Hotel, Stanley Street, Collingwood, about 1862.

A woolwashing jetty at South Yarra; photograph by Charles Nettleton, about 1870.

South-western corner of Brunswick and Gertrude Streets, Fitzroy, 1866. Dr William Crooke's house is on the right.

and rendered extremely susceptible to certain forms of disease, by living in neighbourhoods where miasma prevails.[3]

The *Observer* replied to the Protectionist *Age* thus:

What use . . . to the people of our own district would Protection be if the Pollution Bill remains intact? Through the obstruction offered by the obnoxious clauses of the Public Health Bill, we have already lost, at least, one woollen manufactory, which has been taken to the Barwon; and we know that Mr. Reeves and others are prepared to become something more than 'washers of wool for the English manufacturer', were the obstacles to their doing so removed.

At present, the *Observer* said, any tanner or woolwasher who let any effluent enter the Yarra 'shall be subject to fines and penalties quite sufficient to banish all thought of engaging in manufactories near the Yarra out of the head of any enterprising capitalist'.

While the assault on the pollution clauses was at its height, the *Observer* had visions of the Yarra becoming the Clyde of Victoria: 'The large river frontage of East Collingwood [ought to be] turned to some account . . . We will not despair of seeing wharves and jetties at the foot of Johnston Street and other streets, with steamers and barges alongside.'

The *Observer* (and Thomas Embling in parliament) advocated a government grant of £500 to clear 1,000 dead trees which blocked the Yarra in Collingwood-Richmond, snagging 'all kinds of filth', e.g., dead dogs and cats and refuse from drains. (Refuse from factories was not mentioned.) Another Collingwood parliamentarian, the *Observer* said, had made a similar plea years before, 'but South Yarra was against him'.

Pollution from the Reilly Street open drain in particular was increasing, said the *Observer*, because of the growing population of Carlton and of the Melbourne General Cemetery. (Complaints about cemetery drainage continued for thirty years. This drainage, which flowed through Carlton street channels before entering the Reilly Street drain, allegedly included water pumped from vaults.)

During the 1865 debates, Yarra pollution became related to the issue of air pollution. A proposed health amendment Bill included a new clause (taken, apparently, from a Melbourne City Council by-law) prohibiting brickmaking within a hundred yards of any dwelling other than brickmakers' dwellings. The *Observer* commented:

A most determined crusade is being made against the development of several local industries, which afford employment to hundreds of

I

our humbler fellow citizens . . . Brickmakers, earthenpipe and coarse earthenware manufacturers are, like fellmongers, etc., to be henceforward proscribed from following their lawful callings in the very localities wherein may reside members of the upstart clique which is determined that smoke or stench, from vulgar industries, must not come between the wind and their nobility . . . Laws prejudicial to the real producers of wealth will, however, react upon those who attempt to enforce them; and the repeated attacks made upon the rights of labor, under the cover of the Public Health Bill, will yet raise a storm about the ears of those members of the Civil Service, with whom originate the conspiracy [i.e. the south-of-the-Yarra aristocracy], which they will regret having evoked.[4]

Following objections from East Collingwood, Fitzroy and other councils, the government agreed to drop the clause. In 1871, according to government statistics, East Collingwood had four brickyards, employing forty-six hands (as well as giving casual employment to carriers and others); Fitzroy had one brickyard, employing apparently no wage labour.

Manufacturers, actual or aspiring, were a ubiquitous pressure group. Isaac Reeves in 1865 urged the forming of trade associations 'from end to end of the colony to watch the progress of matters affecting their interest in the legislature'. He himself helped to found a Victorian Manufacturers' Association, largely with Collingwood-Richmond support.

In similar vein, brewer Edward Wild bought an interest in the Collingwood *Observer* in 1866, re-named the paper the *Manufacturer* in 1867 and regularly published articles about factories. But, like other ventures of Wild's, the *Manufacturer* was not a financial success. The previous proprietor of the *Observer*, James Macalpine Tait, took over the *Manufacturer*, restored the name *Observer* and continued publishing it until 1909.

In the late 1860s, Collingwood Council was in a quandary over noxious trades: it needed factories so as to improve land values, increase the municipal revenue, provide employment, attract population, and improve local trade, but it had to cope with mounting public criticism and it had to avoid the expense of sewerage.

The Central Board of Health, which inspected the streets and industries of all suburbs once a year, enormously increased its visits and letters to Collingwood and Richmond in 1868–9. The C.B.H. found new and bigger noxious factories. It also found that an amending Health Act of 1867, which directed the disinfection of all liquid refuse before its discharge from such establishments, was not being enforced by the councils.

Whenever householders complained about new offensive factories arising in their midst, the council refused to intervene until after the nuisance occurred, that is, until the works were fully operating. By then a proprietor had little to fear, especially if he had taken the precaution of becoming a councillor. The classic case is that of James Hobson Turner. He was a city wool broker who had a house and several allotments in Collingwood (in Portions 57, 58, 59). In the 1860s he took over a woolwashing establishment in Portion 60 on lease. In February 1867 he entered the council, and was joined at the council table in June by another fellmongery proprietor, Daniel Ross Hunter. (In July 1868 Hunter resigned from the council after disposing of his business to ex-councillor Thomas Greenwood; Greenwood then secured re-election to the council, unopposed, to occupy Hunter's seat.)

In 1868 a tannery arose on one of Turner's allotments in Portion 57, a quarter of a mile from the Yarra. He leased the premises to associates. Residents petitioned the council against Turner's tannery. The outcome was summed up by Mayor Joseph Bowring (a baker), speaking at a metropolitan conference on Yarra pollution:

> A tannery was started in East Collingwood among a lot of cottages which people had built for themselves, in order to live comfortably on their own land, and when they came to complain to the council of the nuisance in their midst, nothing could be done for them.

As shown by such cases, the machinery of Victoria's public health legislation was defective. Although required by law to employ an inspector of nuisances, the council did not regard this position highly. If the inspector was too conscientious in sanitary matters, he might incur the wrath of guilty persons who controlled his appointment. He could then be dismissed, as was Police Sergeant Nimon (part-time inspector of nuisances) in 1860. If he was a full-time officer, as was the case after 1860, he could be diverted into running messages, collecting revenue (from dog licences or liquor licences), and detecting Sunday trading in hotels. Indeed, some councillors regarded these as being the inspector's chief duties. The inspectorship was often regarded as a sinecure, which a dominant faction might award to one of its outside supporters, as happened in 1864. When the council retrenched during economy drives, it sometimes combined the inspector's duties with those of the overseer of works. Inspectors were not hard to hire: one advertisement attracted sixty-one applicants. (For such reasons, the Central Board of Health preferred the position to be filled part-time by a police sergeant.)

Furthermore, the legal machinery was cumbersome. If a conscientious inspector wished to tackle an offender, he must wait until the next council meeting, must obtain an order from the council to desist, must serve the order personally, and could prosecute only upon disobedience of the order and only with the approval of the council. 'The law is not respected', Collingwood Council reported to the C.B.H. in 1886, 'as people know that action cannot be taken prior to their getting notice.' Again, health laws provided for maximum, not minimum fines, enabling the court (probably consisting of local honorary justices, possibly friends of the defendant) to inflict merely a nominal fine, on the pretext that the offender had begun, even in the smallest way, to remedy the offence.

After Smith Street butcher John Pritchard was let off with a five-shilling fine for persistent backyard slaughtering, Fitzroy solicitor James McKean denounced the partiality of the honorary justices of Fitzroy and East Collingwood. Packed benches were no rarity, he said. The position was similar in Richmond. When an expanding tannery received lenient treatment from Richmond's justices, the itinerant inspector from the Central Board of Health remarked in exasperation: 'I could see . . . that there was a feeling that operated against the conviction of persons prosecuted for the pollution of the Yarra.' As Victorian Attorney-General G. P. Smith put it,

> Richmond and East Collingwood, for the sake of a local benefit, have suffered these manufactories to be established on the banks of the Yarra and have protected persons who violated the law . . . It is of no use to bring these persons before justices, because local interest induces them to disregard their oath of office and they refuse to convict the offenders.[5]

According to the Victorian Municipal Directories for 1875–81, about one-quarter or one-third of the dozen honorary justices in Collingwood were noxious trades proprietors; the remainder were shopkeepers or building contractors. When the Central Board of Health and Melbourne City Council prosecuted a Collingwood market gardener in 1875 for permitting nightmen to dump nightsoil into the Yarra from his land near Johnston Street bridge, the case was heard in Melbourne, not Collingwood, to ensure a conviction. It was universally assumed that Collingwood magistrates would be biased against the city complainants and in favour of the local ratepayer. The *Observer* acknowledged this, but saw nothing wrong with it.

There was not necessarily a conscious conspiracy behind such partiality. The justices were probably doing their duty as they conceived it in the circumstances. They dealt sternly with unrespectable deviants—vagrants, drunks, delinquents, thieves—but saw mitigating circumstances in the case of respectable and industrious gentlemen, pillars of the community, who were doing what was 'normal' in such circles—letting effluent enter an already dirty river.

In 1868 a reformer entered the council. He was Arthur Snowden, aged thirty-nine, a city solicitor and prominent Anglican layman. Snowden had lived since 1858 in picturesque St Hellier's Street (Portion 77) near the Yarra, and was concerned about the deterioration of the Yarra and the Flat. He immediately revived the council's defunct health sub-committee, and insisted that in future the committee's reports should be discussed at length at each council meeting. He demanded a clean-up of the abattoirs, and supported residents of the Flat in protesting against Councillor Turner's tannery.

Snowden clashed head-on with the council on the issue of Yarra pollution. On the motion of tanner Turner, the council decided that the local parliamentary representatives should again seek the immediate repeal of the Yarra pollution legislation. According to the *Argus*, Turner 'had no better reason to offer for so doing than his belief that the establishment of a number of manufactories would increase the borough revenue, and a statement that the Yarra had not been for years what could be called a pure river'. Snowden was the only dissentient to this motion; his alternative motion (that the government be asked to abolish the offensive factories, with compensation to the owners) found no seconder and was received with laughter. The *Argus* published an editorial in support of Snowden, warning, *inter alia*, that if the Yarra became increasingly an industrial sewer, 'all its solid elements will be precipitated, and will form a deposit of putrefying mud, evolving poisonous gases so often as it is laid bare to the sun by contraction of the water in the channel', resulting in 'the speedy destruction, by atmospheric poisoning, of the inhabitants of Collingwood and Richmond flats'.[6]

Hopelessly outnumbered, Snowden left the council after a year, and went on to bigger things. In the 1890s he entered Melbourne

City Council, was three times mayor, received a knighthood, and entered the Legislative Council. He became a member of the executive council of the Australasian Federation League.

Each noxious trades proprietor who joined East Collingwood Council from the late 1860s onwards usually seemed to do so amid public complaints about his particular business. For example, in May 1869 residents of Portion 61 complained to the council and the Central Board of Health about fumes from Dr William Crooke's brick kilns. At the next council election, in August, Crooke secured the seat being vacated by Arthur Snowden, but withdrew after two months. A second brickmaker was a councillor in 1870–3 and a third in 1874–7. When residents of Portion 61 complained in 1871 about yet another brickmaker beginning operations there, the council predictably replied that it was 'unable' to interfere until the establishment was proved to be a nuisance. Meanwhile, in the 1870s William Crooke became a member of the Central Board of Health. Thus, if householders complained to either the council or the C.B.H., a brickmaker was on hand to help deal with the complaint. In the 1880s, as the brick industry moved to new holes in outer suburbs, the old brick-holes of East Collingwood became private garbage dumps. Crooke then sold vacant allotments in Portion 61 to a building society which built workers' cottages.

During 1869, residents of Portion 54 complained about nuisances arising from the Glasshouse tannery and boot factory in Rokeby Street. The new proprietor, city leather merchant Hugh Thomson, was reluctant to rectify the matter; in August 1870 he became a councillor for three years.

Early in 1869 Melbourne City Council decided to ask the government to give the City Council complete control over the Yarra from Dight's Falls, Clifton Hill, to the river's mouth. This would supplant the authority shared by nine suburban councils from Collingwood to Williamstown. The riverside councils took alarm, and held a conference (which the City Council did not attend) to see what could be done about the mounting public criticism of Yarra pollution. During these discussions it was pointed out that the City Council was not acting from completely altruistic motives —that Collingwood and Richmond were Protectionist strongholds and had encouraged factories, while the City of Melbourne was the centre of Free Trade interests.

In March 1869, at the insistence of the Central Board of Health, the council served notices on noxious trades proprietors—brewers, tanners, fellmongers—requiring them to install within one month (in accordance with the 1867 amending Health Act) a tank for filtering and deodorizing fluid refuse before discharging it into street channels or into the Yarra. But the council did nothing more than merely serve the notices, and the proprietors ignored these. Of thirteen proprietors listed, five were former councillors, one (Turner) was still in the council and one (Hugh Thomson) entered the council a year later.

The council was particularly tolerant of Councillor Turner's two establishments. In July 1869 when Councillor Snowden's health sub-committee recommended serving notices on the noxious trades proprietors for having failed to provide the required filter tanks, the council struck Turner's name off the list. In August 1869 Turner became mayor, symbolizing the real trend of the times in Collingwood. The council's medical officer, Dr A. Livingstone, complained to the council about a smell from Turner's works, but the council took no official action; it merely requested Turner privately to abate the nuisance, and he ignored the request.

The C.B.H. instigated the appointment in 1870 of a Royal Commission on noxious trades. The C.B.H. chairman, Dr William McCrac, who was one of Victoria's leading exponents of the miasma theory of disease, became chairman of the Royal Commission. The Commission's reports, drafted by McCrae, demanded an end to river and air pollution. The Commission believed that the Yarra above the city 'should be a fine stream of pure drinking water, available to our citizens for the healthy recreations of bathing and boating. [Its] banks should afford a pleasant promenade.' The Commission recommended that Collingwood and Richmond be allowed to keep their riverside factories, but that a sewer be constructed, running parallel with the Yarra, from Reilly Street, Collingwood, to near the mouth of the Yarra. This would carry off the contents of the street drains of Collingwood and Richmond and all liquid refuse from the riverside factories and abattoirs. It would become the nucleus of an eventual sewerage system for Melbourne. Meanwhile, all fluid refuse from the factories should be drained into precipitating tanks and deodorized; only purified fluid was to be allowed into the Yarra; the solid residue was to be carried away. Fellmongers were to be forced to remove their washing jetties from the river.

To minimize air pollution, the Commission recommended: that all organic raw materials (e.g., skin, bones, entrails) be stored under cover and processed promptly; that all solid wastes be deodorized and carted away daily; and that the vapours of the boiling of animal matter be conducted through the furnace before passing into the air.

The Royal Commission's reports evoked a hostile reaction from the noxious trades community. One member of the Commission, Collingwood fellmonger G. D. Gill (of Portion 59), rejected the final report and resigned, apparently (said McCrae) because the Commission's recommendation would prevent fellmongers occupying half the width of the river for washing wool.

The publicity of the Royal Commission stimulated a temporary improvement in the conduct of the riverside factories, but by the mid-1870s the old laxity had returned. The C.B.H. continued to complain to the council about Councillor Turner's works, demanding a prosecution for Yarra pollution. The council parried, stating that if ever the government provided a better location for such industries, the council would be pleased to remove them from Collingwood. Turner was mayor again in 1877 and served a total of fifteen years in the council. In the 1880s he prospered as a land speculator.

Another noxious trades proprietor who made a mark on Collingwood Council was Henry Walker, the soap and candle manufacturer of Portions 62 and 63. Walker told the 1870 Royal Commission that, because of smells from his factories, he had suffered from public opinion. In 1872 he became a councillor. Later he attributed his entry into municipal politics to woolwasher Peter Nettleton. Henry Walker was a councillor for twelve years and mayor for five. During this time, residents of Kew continued to complain to the council about Walker's fumes—unsuccessfully. They also approached the Central Board of Health, which referred them back to the council. The Kew residents subscribed £200 to take legal action, but found that proceedings could be taken only by the council.

The council's attitude to air pollution was inconsistent. When the government in 1874 proposed to build a contagious diseases hospital at Fairfield, adjoining Clifton Hill, Collingwood councillors objected that winds would 'carry contagious gases all over Collingwood'.

Into the 1880s the Central Board of Health continued complaining about the permissiveness on the part of Collingwood and Richmond councils, and vainly urged the government to implement the 1870 recommendations. The factories discharging into the Yarra increased in number and size. In 1892 Collingwood was still Victoria's second biggest centre for tanning, fellmongering and woolwashing, being surpassed somewhat by Richmond. Collingwood's eight establishments, mostly equipped with steam, employed 108 persons. Annually they tanned 18,640 hides and 25,600 skins, and washed 1,185,104 pounds of wool.

After 1871 noxious factories—including a tannery, several woolwasheries and an ammonia factory—arose even in Reilly Street, Clifton Hill, as much as a mile from the Yarra. The career of one of these industrialists—woolwasher Robert Hall—may be taken as an example. He had experience in Yorkshire in two trades: wool-dressing and cabinetmaking. Reaching Melbourne in 1863, he worked as a carpenter; in his spare time he constructed a patent woolscouring machine, which he later manufactured and installed in about twenty sheep stations. His Reilly Street woolwashery, established about 1871, became one of the most productive in Victoria. Hall sold out for a big price in 1888, and during his retirement he served as a Collingwood councillor.

The new Reilly Street factories received council permission to discharge sewage into the Reilly Street open drain. When residents and a section of the council protested, councillors Turner and Walker replied that factories were 'beneficial to the district'. Other industries using the drain included a private slaughterhouse (where blood from sheep's throats flowed directly into the drain), the Collingwood gasworks and later a Clifton Hill brewery. The council asked the government for funds to cover the drain, thereby putting the pollution out of sight, but this was not done until the end of the century.

And so, partly because of this industrial development and partly because of suburban sprawl, the Yarra became dirtier. After the 1880s, various 'improvement' works were implemented along the river's entire course, but these consisted largely of denuding its banks and straightening its course, so that the street and industrial drainage of the metropolis might be more speedily shifted to Port Phillip Bay. The Yarra's dirtiness, contrasting with the more obvious beauty of Sydney's harbour, became a national joke. It became forgotten that the Yarra was once drinkable and that its dirtiness was man-made.

The conflict between city and suburbs over the use of the Yarra overlaps with another controversy—about proposals for sewerage and for a metropolitan board of works. This is discussed in the next chapter.

Yarra pollution is still a problem today. Whereas nineteenth-century pollution was largely organic, the main worry now is from industrial chemicals. For example, patches of oil often appear. The culprits are not always factories. In 1970 an oil spill was traced to a building in Collingwood owned by a Victorian government instrumentality. The building has an oil-operated water heater in the basement. Unknown to the council, the heater's emergency overflow-pipe had been connected to an underground storm-water drain, which led straight to the Yarra.

Air pollution, too, is a continuing story. Throughout the metropolis, factories break Victoria's air pollution regulations every day. They blatantly exceed the maximum fifteen-minute time limit allowed by the regulations for their first firing of the morning and any necessary re-firing during the production day. Some factories disguise their offence by emitting most of their fumes at night and by colouring them white. The Victorian Health Department and the suburban councils are reluctant to prosecute factories because of the manpower and legal expenses involved. They rely instead on a policy of inspections and quiet persuasion. Meanwhile, factories continue their present practices.

Because of its material growth, the Borough of East Collingwood qualified for elevation in status in 1873 as the Town of Colling-wood (dropping the prefix 'East') and in 1876 as the City of Colling-wood. By then, as shown in the previous two chapters, it was being made into a good place for resourceful men to develop capital. In this chapter and the next, we shall see to what extent it was being made into a good place for people to live.

Some idea of the human condition can be gained from census statistics concerning animals. Despite its relatively large popula-tion, Collingwood long retained a barnyard atmosphere. Livestock

TABLE 8

Livestock and poultry, 1871 and 1891, compared with population and dwellings

	1871		1891	
	C'wood	*Fitzroy*	*C'wood*	*Fitzroy*
Population	18,598	15,547	35,070	32,452
Inhabited dwellings	4,013	3,020	7,141	6,174
Livestock:				
Horses	787	949	1,832	1,614
Cattle (inc. milch cows)	320	205	290	188
Sheep	482	268	65	4
Pigs	290	69	60	—
Goats	376	209	111	42
Asses, mules	2	2	2	1
Total	2,257	1,702	2,360	1,849
Poultry:				
Geese	471	268	281	224
Ducks	3,902	2,049	3,057	1,705
Fowls	18,195	13,461	23,723	18,008
Turkeys	108	124	136	149
Other	4	12	12	5
Total	22,680	15,914	27,209	20,091

(horses, cattle, sheep, pigs and goats) were kept in 1871 by 17 per cent of Collingwood's householders, and poultry (geese, ducks, fowls and turkeys) were kept by 36 per cent, with similar figures in Fitzroy. In total numbers, Collingwood had far more animals than Fitzroy (indeed, more even than rural Hawthorn, across the Yarra). In Fitzroy the human inhabitants in 1871 were beginning to draw level with the number of animals, but in Collingwood animals still outnumbered humans four to three. Collingwood was a barnyard crowded with people. (The details are shown in Table 8.)

The two municipalities also differed significantly in the kind of animals kept. If we calculate the number of animals for every hundred dwellings in 1871, we find:

	horses	cattle	sheep	pigs	goats	geese	ducks	fowls	turkeys
C'wood	20	8	12	7	9	12	97	454	3
Fitzroy	32	7	5	2	7	9	68	448	4

In livestock, Fitzroy surpassed Collingwood only in horses, a fact in keeping with Fitzroy's superior dwellings, pavements and social standing. The categories of livestock in which Collingwood excelled—cattle, sheep, pigs and goats—were associated more with mud, vacant allotments, garbage and noxious trades. In poultry, Fitzroy surpassed Collingwood only in turkeys, which were presumably considered superior to fowls.

Between 1871 and 1891, with increasing urbanization, animal statistics changed significantly. First in Fitzroy, then in Collingwood, people began to outnumber livestock and poultry. In both places, population doubled, while livestock numbers remained steady and poultry increased by about one-quarter; among livestock, horses doubled; cattle (comprising chiefly milch cows) decreased slightly; and, probably because of the suppression of some nuisances, especially at butchers' shops, sheep, pigs and goats decreased sharply. Among poultry, fowls multiplied at the expense of geese and ducks. The increase in the number of dwellings no doubt resulted in an increase also in the number of domestic pets (dogs, cats, caged birds); if these are added to livestock and poultry (at the rate of one pet per house), then humans in Collingwood (though not in Fitzroy) were still outnumbered by animals even in 1891.

Increasingly the keeping of animals became recognized as a

problem. In the 1860s the council prohibited cattle and goats from wandering in streets or vacant land south of Reilly Street and began registering dogs. Thereafter the sanitary inspector had to conduct a regular animal round-up.

By the end of the 1860s Collingwood was under increasing public scrutiny not only because of its noxious trades but also because of its general hygiene. Victoria experienced a cholera scare in 1866, a smallpox outbreak in 1869; it also had periodic epidemics of typhoid, diphtheria, scarlet fever and measles—all frequently fatal. Amendments to Victoria's public health legislation in 1867 gave councils a little more power to enforce the removal of accumulated filth from privies, backyards, stables, cowsheds, pigsties, abattoirs and streets, but some councils (including Collingwood) were slow to act. Following a suspected case of smallpox at Collingwood in 1869, the Melbourne *Herald* commented:

> East Collingwood . . . is a complete magnet of attraction for fever and death. Sanitary regulations are utterly ignored within its boundaries; the streets are seldom cleaned . . . The backyards . . . are seldom, if ever, examined by an inspector of nuisances. In some of them the keeping of swine is quite common . . . If once the fell disease of smallpox fixes itself in East Collingwood, there will be no stamping out possible, and it will throw out branch lines of easy communication with the more aristocratic dwellings of East Melbourne, and the middle class homes of Fitzroy. If the East Collingwood councillors be remiss, careless or incapable, then the government ought to put them on one side, and perform the necessary work, so that the valuable lives of our working classes may not be sacrificed.

The council replied that it spent £9 a week on maintaining streets and channels, and £13 a week cleaning them, to which someone retorted: 'The money may be paid out of the borough funds, but does the council see that the work is done for the money?'[1] The council claimed that no serious disease was prevalent in Collingwood other than 'the ordinary type of colonial fever' (probably meaning typhoid fever) which it accepted as 'normal'. But the Central Board of Health reported in 1874: 'Medical men in many instances do not recognize the characters of true typhoid. True typhoid fever is more prevalent in this colony than is generally imagined.'

However, apparently to make up for its tolerance of noxious trades, the council in the early 1870s was at last attempting a clean-up of streets and private premises. It publicly displayed 500 copies of new by-laws (drafted by the C.B.H.), sprayed disinfectants in gutters and ordered property owners to fill in stagnant pools.

The Central Board of Health pressed the council to tackle the pig nuisance. Collingwood then had 290 pigs—four times as many as Fitzroy and even 17 pigs more than rural Hawthorn. From 1871 the council prohibited pig-keeping in the most densely populated region (south of Reilly Street and west of Hoddle Street), but some pig-owners ignored this for several years. The council continued to tolerate a large piggery attached to butcher Charles Alexander's boiling-down works in Ramsden Street, Clifton Hill (see p. 92), despite complaints from residents about pigs wandering around streets there. Judging from the municipal ratebook, Alexander had land dealings with some influential citizens including (in 1872) Councillor James H. Turner, the noxious trades proprietor (see p. 115). Not until 1880 did the council prohibit pig-keeping everywhere in the municipality. Even so, Collingwood in 1891 still had sixty pigs—three times as many as Hawthorn; Fitzroy had none.

Throughout the 1870s the council plodded along with its construction of footpaths. Streets on the Flat received a scattering of gravel free. Shopkeepers could lay flagstones at their own cost, with the council paying half the cost when funds became available. After 1872 the shopkeepers tended to switch to the new asphalt paving, which was being promoted by city contractor James Shephard's Patent Composition Paving Company Limited. Combining waste coal-tar from gasworks with broken bluestone, asphalt was cheaper than flagging and better than gravel. It was opposed by some cynics who ridiculed the failure of early experiments and by some interests who saw no benefit in it for themselves. In the late 1870s the council laid asphalt footpaths throughout the Slope, began testing asphalt for road surfacing in Smith Street and introduced mechanization by acquiring a road steam-roller. Streets on the Flat were still being kerbed and channelled, and had to wait longer for asphalt. The council also gradually constructed back lanes, charging the cost to owners; but the owners frequently delayed and evaded payment.

As in the 1860s, the disposal of night-soil was still a major problem (see chapter 5).

In 1871 the council was under pressure from the Central Board of Health to act against leaky cesspits, as required by the 1867 legislation and as the City of Melbourne was currently doing. Melbourne City Council in 1870–1 offered one free emptying for every cesspit; it thus detected all defective cesspits, filled them in and began operating a free weekly pan-emptying service. The Central Board of Health approved, although it really preferred either sewerage or the earth closet (because the earth acted as a deodorant). City houses built thereafter had neither a cesspit nor a pipe for overflow into street channels. Collingwood Council, like most others, was apathetic but, to pacify the Central Board, it half-heartedly issued orders against several cesspits.

In 1874 a Melbourne firm of nightmen, Hesse and Rummel, involved Collingwood councillors in a scheme for transforming the collection and disposal of Collingwood's night-soil into a lucrative industry. Hesse and Rummel had patented a process for distilling night-soil into a marketable concentrated manure. They proposed operating at the Collingwood manure depot, where they would purchase the raw materials from Collingwood and Fitzroy nightmen for two shillings a load. Hesse and Rummel formed the Collingwood Poudrette (Guano) and Amonia Company Limited, and recruited as large shareholders three Collingwood councillors —Henry Walker and Joseph Bowring (each having 100 £1 shares) and Charles Morgan (50 shares). Other shareholders included the council's surveyor-engineer (10 shares), a Fitzroy councillor (25 shares) and two former Fitzroy councillors (150 shares and 25 shares), as well as members of the public (10 to 50 shares each). (This financial interest of the councillors is not mentioned in the *Observer* in 1875 and was presumably not known to the public; the interest was discovered in the Defunct Companies Records in the State Archives during the research for this book.) On the motion of shareholders Walker and Morgan, Collingwood Council granted the company a long lease (fourteen years) of a portion of the Collingwood manure depot at low rental (initially ten shillings a week) and evicted the existing tenants (Draper and Son, competitors of Hesse and Rummel).[2]

The poudrette project failed after a year. According to Hesse, the reason was that until late 1875 Collingwood and Fitzroy Councils failed to enforce the law respecting watertight cesspits, and that therefore the night-soil sent to the works frequently contained an immense proportion of mere water, which had to be removed by evaporation at great expense. These engineering difficulties doubled the cost of the works. Lacking funds, Hesse and Rummel sold the works to one of the shareholders (Councillor Charles Morgan, mayor of Collingwood) and moved to the southern suburbs, where they used portable pans. The mayor then increased the poudrette project's income (but also its smells) by treating blood from the Collingwood abattoirs. When complaints about smells came from travellers along the Heidelberg Road and from Yarra Bend Asylum, the C.B.H. ordered that the works (situated on Crown land) be closed. From Collingwood's viewpoint, this was yet another instance of non-Collingwood interests seeking to stifle native industry.

The decline of the cesspit system in Collingwood began in October 1875 when several circumstances combined to warrant action.

Some of the circumstances were of Victoria-wide significance. Two Collingwood nightmen were suffocated in a cesspit at East Melbourne. While inside the cesspit (measuring 6½ ft deep, 8 ft long and 5 ft wide) bailing it out, they apparently inhaled fumes from a deodorant—carbonic acid. The coroner said that he had previously held inquests on a total of four children gassed or drowned in cesspits. The coroner (and editorial writers) said that legislative action against the very existence of cesspits was long overdue.[3] The coroner attributed the delay to successive changes of government; with each new ministry, the previously prepared health Bill perished and a fresh copy had to be supplied. The *Argus* added a further reason for the delay: 'Several attempts have been made to obtain legislative authority [but] the owners of city property are highly influential, and hitherto they have succeeded in averting any [such] legislation . . . that would have entailed upon them some little inconvenience and perhaps some little expense.' Then Melbourne experienced a scarlet fever epidemic, the worst for that disease since January 1861. Metropolitan deaths from scarlet fever, which for the previous five years had averaged only 3 a month, rose to 19 in August 1875, 60 in September, 179 in October, and a peak of 251 in November (compared with a peak of 73 in January 1861). As scarlet fever was considered a 'miasmatic' disease, the government finally agreed to empower metropolitan councils from April 1876 to fill up *any* unhealthy-looking cesspit, leaking or not, and to prohibit any new cesspit.

Unexpectedly, Collingwood Council became one of the foremost exponents of the new law. Several circumstances, in addition to those already cited, help to explain this conversion.

Firstly, 1875 was a crisis year for Collingwood's night-soil disposal system. Dumping night-soil in the Yarra was made clearly illegal with severe penalties; neighbouring shires decided that they

View of Collingwood from the Johnston Street bridge, 1867.

Smith Street, complete with cable trams and telephone poles in the late 1880s; looking south, with Collingwood on the left and Fitzroy on the right.

Victoria Brewery, Victoria Parade, East Melbourne, 1888.

would not allow 'foreign' night-soil within their bounds; and the Poudrette Company was refusing to receive night-soil from cess-pits unless the householders undertook to fill the pits in and use pans. 'Every cesspit in Fitzroy and Collingwood', said the *Observer*, 'is overflowing.'

Secondly, Collingwood Council came to realize that cesspit banning was cheaper than other methods of municipal sanitary reform. An outbreak of scarlet fever in a house in James Street (Portion 56) had presented the council with a dilemma. The family was being attended by Dr William Crooke, a member of the Central Board of Health.* Crooke and the C.B.H. each wrote to the council, demanding improvements to the street's dirty gutters. The *Observer*, defending the council, commented that the small ratepayers of James Street and other muddy alleys were making capital out of scarlet fever and were coercing the council into im-proving their worthless property at the municipality's expense. The council solved the James Street problem by condemning the in-fected house as unfit for habitation and by successfully prosecuting the owner-occupier for having an overflowing cesspit. Obviously it was cheaper for the council if the onus of maintaining hygiene was borne by individual householders instead of by the municipality.

Thus at the height of all the crises of 1875, even before the anti-cesspit Bill became law, the council (on the motion of Councillor Henry Walker of the Poudrette Company) began ordering that the worst cesspits be replaced by pans. During November and Decem-ber nightmen were emptying and abolishing about 30 Collingwood cesspits a week, and had a waiting-list of 200. Henceforth the pan system gradually became general in Collingwood. Some house-holders voluntarily joined the trend; but the council still needed to serve 'fill-up' notices until the end of the century. In the late

* Dr Crooke's treatment for both scarlet fever and diphtheria was to admin-ister successively an emetic, an aperient, quinine, champagne and (most important of all, he said) mineral spa water. The mineral water, he said, 'appears to give the constitution the power of resistance to the progress of the disease . . . For a considerable time, I have abandoned all treatment save the use of this mineral water. In severe cases of wasting diseases in children, I have cured several cases by its use alone . . . I put it by the bedside at night, so that they can drink it whenever they like; it quenches the thirst in the most remark-able way in its natural state, and is very refreshing.' (From Crooke's evidence to the Royal Commission on Diphtheria, 1872.) Crooke's treatment was probably neither better nor worse than other treatments at this time. To cure diphtheria, the *Observer* in 1866 recommended taking patients to the Collingwood gasworks to inhale the coal-tar fumes. Later, Crooke was said to be the first Australian practitioner to draw attention to diseased milk as a factor in diphtheria.

1870s, these orders were being made at the rate of about ten a month.

After the failure of the Poudrette Company, the council reluctantly followed the example of other councils in superintending night-soil collection throughout the municipality. However, unlike the City of Melbourne, Collingwood Council declined to finance the service from rates. It was pointed out that in Collingwood a sanitary rate would fall heavily upon ratepayers whose property had a high valuation, and would therefore strike opposition; furthermore, Collingwood had many vacant allotments, and these did not need the service. So, for the remainder of the century, Collingwood operated an optional system. Householders could engage a low-tendering contractor nominated by the council (charging in the 1880s about fifteen shillings per year), or they could engage a superior, more expensive, 'private' nightman (e.g., Draper or Hesse) who supplied earth or chemical disinfectants. The council's health officer complained that allowing a choice of nightmen in Collingwood was a grave mistake, as in some streets the work was carried on every night in the week. And there were some disreputable householders who, particularly in depression times, emptied night-soil into street channels; if fined, they often could not afford to pay and preferred to go to gaol.

A study of Collingwood sanitation can help us to understand the development not only of Collingwood but also of metropolitan Melbourne—for example, the coming of metropolitan sewerage. Why was sewerage delayed for five decades until the end of the century? Some possible general contributing factors are already well known: e.g., low-density suburban sprawl made sewerage more costly in Melbourne than elsewhere, and cholera, which provided an impetus overseas, was absent in Victoria. A study of Collingwood suggests that one factor deserving emphasis is tension between Melbourne City Council and the suburban councils, notably Collingwood Council.

In 1874 the City Council convened conferences of metropolitan councils at Melbourne Town Hall to discuss proposals to establish a metropolitan board of works. The board, comprising representatives from the councils, would manage certain affairs for the metropolis, including undertakings that were big and costly (water, sewerage and gas) and matters requiring co-operation and uniformity (harbour and river improvement, regulation of noxious trades, parks and hackney carriages). Collingwood Council, which had just become committed to the poudrette project, was one of the first councils to reject the scheme, and even boycotted some of the discussions. For the next twelve years Melbourne City Council tried to overcome the opposition or apathy of suburban councils.

Collingwood opponents of the board proposal had several fears. Firstly, they said, the board would result in additional taxation being imposed on property-owners. Furthermore, the City Council would dominate the board and would use it to defeat Collingwood and Richmond on the issue of river pollution. The *Observer* in 1874 had no faith in any scheme involving Melbourne's town clerk E. G. FitzGibbon. FitzGibbon, the paper said, was angry about Collingwood's opposition to the scheme and was fulminating about Collingwood's river pollution. The paper added that Collingwood's new member of parliament, G. D. Langridge, intended to introduce legislation to open up the Yarra for manufacturing, and that this move would further annoy FitzGibbon. The *Observer* also objected that the municipal councillors who would comprise the board were amateurs and that, being responsible for such a wide range of services, the board would be unwieldy. Harbour maintenance, for example, was worth a board of its own, comprising a small group of experts.

In 1883 both Collingwood and Fitzroy again declined to co-operate with the board proposal. When the Melbourne *Argus* criticized this attitude on the part of such 'important centres of population', the *Observer* denounced the *Argus* as 'the mouthpiece of the would-be Melbourne monopolists'. The *Observer* said:

> The composition of the board gives such a preponderance of representation to the Melbourne corporation that the interests of Fitzroy and Collingwood would be virtually ignored. Melbourne demands eleven members, allotting only two each to Fitzroy and Collingwood. The latter places would be rated the same as Melbourne yet there is but little doubt that Melbourne would absorb the greater bulk of the money.[4]

Fitzroy and Collingwood, argued the *Observer*, were already well-drained—Fitzroy by natural means and Collingwood by underground drains; indeed they were ahead of Melbourne in drainage, and so they should not be called upon to subsidize Melbourne. Repeating its criticism of 1874 about the amateur composition of the board and about the machinations of FitzGibbon, the *Observer* said that FitzGibbon was trying to supplant representative institutions—the local councils—with a bureaucratic machine.

The Collingwood *Mercury*, however, took a different view; it supported the board proposal and criticized 'the short-sighted policy of these councils who have held aloof from the movement instead of assisting in maturing it by sending their best men to represent them who would have insisted on an equitable system of taxation and representation'.

The impasse over the board of works proposal lasted for another three years. Then the unexpected happened. When the proposal was again put to metropolitan councils in 1886, it was viewed with increasing favour, even in Collingwood. Late in 1887, Collingwood Council endorsed the proposal. What were the circumstances surrounding Collingwood's conversion? As we shall see, some of the circumstances related to the metropolis in general, while some were peculiar to Collingwood.

Firstly Collingwood, like other inner suburbs, was having increasing difficulty in disposing of night-soil. In 1880 the Department of Lands and Survey forced the closure of the Collingwood manure depot, following complaints about night-soil percolating from trenches into the Yarra.

The night-soil collected by Collingwood's contractor was supposed to go to farms ten miles away, beyond Preston, to be afterwards ploughed in. Occasionally farmers might pay 1s 6d to 2s 6d a load—an incentive to proper disposal. However, usually (e.g., when crops were in) there was little demand for night-soil; and the distances, the long hours of work (sixteen hours nightly, six nights a week) and the crushing weight ($2\frac{1}{2}$ tons, including the cart) were a temptation to release half, or all, of the load along the road. Some carters boasted of their cleverness in lightening their load in this manner. Unlike Fitzroy which made some pretence of a check, neither Collingwood Council nor its contractor checked to see how much, if any, of each load reached its proper destination. No wonder that outer municipalities put restrictions on the passage of inner municipalities' nightcarts. In 1886 the problem of night-soil disposal was discussed at a conference of metropolitan municipalities convened by the Central Board of Health. The conference recommended that the pan system be improved by universally using a deodorizer-disinfectant and by transporting the deodorized night-soil in railway tankers to a site outside the metropolis for further manurial treatment. However, no practical result followed, and the C.B.H. concluded that a voluntary union by metropolitan councils in a comprehensive scheme was hopeless.

It would be unwise to emphasize too strongly the problem of night-soil disposal as a factor in Collingwood Council's conversion to the board of works proposal. As shown in earlier chapters, Collingwood had lived in the shadow of its own dung-heap for a whole generation without much misgiving. To convert Collingwood now, additional incentives were necessary.

A second circumstance was Victoria's increasing concern about epidemic diseases. The main killers were diarrhoeal diseases, typhoid, diphtheria and croup, whooping cough and (to a lesser extent) measles and scarlatina. According to Collingwood figures, half the deaths were of infants in their first year. A brief outbreak of smallpox occurred in 1884, with Collingwood's seven fatalities being typical of the suburbs. What alarmed the public most were the two so-called 'filth diseases'—typhoid and diphtheria—which, judged by mortality figures, increased during the 1880s and reached peaks in 1889 and 1890 respectively. Between 15 and 25 per cent of typhoid fever cases were fatal, and between 30 and 40 per cent of diphtheria cases. In 1886, for example, Collingwood had twelve deaths from typhoid; this suggests a total of about sixty patients for the year.

Judged by mortality statistics and by world standards, Collingwood in the 1880s was not a remarkably unhealthy place. Collingwood's death rate in the 1880s (19 to 21 per thousand inhabitants) was about the same as the rates for the City of Melbourne or for the whole metropolitan area. These rates were about the same as London's (20) and were lower than those of unhealthy English towns such as Manchester (29) and Liverpool (26), but were higher than the rates for Victoria (14 to 17) and for the whole of England (19), and were therefore high enough to warrant concern.

The abolition of Collingwood's cesspits accelerated in the 1880s, apparently reaching a peak with typhoid. The number of fill-up orders made annually by the council increased from 'several' in 1884 to about fifty in 1888.

We must be careful not to measure this concern in twentieth-century terms. Collingwood in 1886 was accustomed to such scourges, just as we are accustomed to road fatalities today. 'Since my last report', wrote the council's sanitary inspector, 'nothing of importance has occurred'; yet he went on to say with unintended irony: 'Cases of typhoid fever are daily being brought under my notice.' The inspector visited the victims' houses, and ordered any filth to be cleaned up, but 'in most cases', he said, 'I find little to complain of'.

A third circumstance concerning attitudes to sanitation was the development of new theories of disease, superseding the miasmatic approach. In the 1870s and 1880s the contagion theory, which had once been generally accepted only for diseases rare in Australia (leprosy, plague, smallpox and cholera), was extended (e.g., by a Melbourne physician, William Thomson, as early as 1874) to cover a major Australian disease: typhoid fever. Simultaneously, the modern germ theory emerged, covering diseases in general. As eventually understood by the end of the century, the new theories meant that typhoid fever was not caught by inhaling a miasma but by consuming water, milk or food that contained microscopic organisms originating from the excreta of a typhoid fever carrier or patient (possibly transmitted, it was realized later, by flies). However, the new theories were slow in taking root in Victoria; they were rejected by most Victorian medical men in the 1870s and were still imperfectly understood in the 1880s. The Collingwood *Mercury* in 1880 endorsed the theories in an editorial urging readers to put earth or ashes in their closet pans as a deodorizer:

> There is nothing so calculated to spread the germs of typhoid fever as these pans . . . Dr Thomson has, in our opinion, clearly proved that typhoid fever is contagious . . . and that the dejecta of typhoid patients polluting water in the slightest degree has excited epidemics of typhoid fever.

But the writer was still influenced by miasmatic thinking, for he added that contagion could also travel through the air: hence the need to use earth or ashes in cesspans.

Even the Central Board of Health was for long confused. In 1885 the C.B.H. was still speaking, though less confidently, about 'miasmatic diseases' such as typhoid ('typhoid is the result of the absorption into the blood of a specific poison generated by vegetable decomposition') and diarrhoea ('many medical men consider that diarrhoea often results from the use of fruit during the summer months, but probably the weather has more to do with it than fruit'). At last, in 1886, the C.B.H. spoke of typhoid fever 'germs', and said that the contagion theory of typhoid fever was now generally accepted.[5] The germ theory was still imperfectly understood among the public; in 1889 some Collingwood residents complained about a nearby rubbish dump and attributed 'numerous cases of typhoid fever' to 'nothing else but the offensive smells arising therefrom'. Nevertheless, it is reasonable to expect that an awareness of germs would contribute to the development of a new perspective on the cost of removing filth from the urban environment. According to American urban historians, the germ theory (together with typhoid) had this effect in towns in the U.S.A.[6]

Some further circumstances, possibly relevant to policies on sanitation, are worth noting. The population boom of the 1880s, and the increasing population density in inner suburbs, meant that sewerage costs would be shared more evenly. The development of suburban cable tramways about 1885 provided precedents for massive excavation works. The emergence of new outer suburbs lessened the relative importance of the City Council in any metropolitan project. And what was the relation of sewerage to the land boom? There is need and scope for a research project to examine these questions in detail in Melbourne and suburbs.

It is difficult to measure the extent to which Collingwood Council was influenced by any of the circumstances noted above. The council made its decisions in the context of attitudes expressed by the government, by other councils and by ratepayers. It must suffice to say that in 1886 Collingwood councillors began to notice some favourable aspects of the proposals for a board of works. For example, the board would tackle the night-soil disposal problem; if the government permitted the board to take over revenue from the Yan Yean water supply system, this might lead to cheaper water rates; and it seemed likely that Melbourne City Council's representation on the board was to be limited to one-fifth. Judging from *Observer* reports, typhoid fever and germs were not explicitly a major consideration in Collingwood Council discussions, although, of course, the importance of these things may have been taken for granted.

The board of works became an issue at Collingwood's annual municipal election in August 1887. Two former councillors, seeking re-election, argued against the proposal. William Smith, building contractor, said that Collingwood had spent a fortune in constructing an 'almost perfect drainage system', and an outside body was now threatening to tax Collingwood to drain other places. Hugh Thomson, tanner, said that the board would only fetter Collingwood, which would have little say on the board. However, both Smith and Thomson were defeated. Weeks later, both Collingwood and Fitzroy councils endorsed the government's Board of Works Bill. In Collingwood only two councillors dissented; one said that, although the board was to receive revenue from the Yan Yean water, it proposed to levy a rate of sixpence in the pound on local property; the other said that he would support the Bill later if the government handed over the Yan Yean system free of charge. The majority, largely newcomers to the council, knew little of the Bill other than that it promised cheap water and removal of night-soil without domination by Melbourne. The other functions originally envisaged for the board (supervision of rivers, noxious trades, parks and public transport) were forgotten. When the Board of Works was finally created in 1890, it was limited to water and sewerage.

During the long wait in the 1890s for the completion of Melbourne's sewerage system, Collingwood was one of the least progressive municipalities in its system of night-soil collection. Collingwood continued to rely on the old open-pan system, whereby each pan was emptied into an open dray and was then replaced, uncleaned and undeodorized, in the closet. After 1888 other suburbs and towns gradually adopted the double-pan system, whereby the full pan was carted away with a sealed lid, and was replaced with a disinfected empty pan. This system had advantages: it was hygienic; it could operate in the daytime; and it checked the nightmen's tendency to spill their load. An alleged disadvantage was its cost—about £1 5s per annum for a weekly service in 1889, slightly more than the open-pan service. Several times Collingwood's inspector and its medical officer of health both recommended the change, but the council resisted. Originally Collingwood expected to be sewered in 1897, but completion was delayed until 1903.

Although Melbourne was in other respects a comparatively progressive city in world terms, there was nothing extraordinarily early about its introduction of sewerage. It was several decades behind London, for example. London made cesspools illegal in 1847, although it then made the mistake of making sewage flow directly into the Thames in the middle of London. A proper sewerage system for London, with an outfall well downstream, was constructed in the early 1860s. (On the other hand, Melbourne beat London in water supply. Melbourne had a clean, continuous and publicly owned water supply in 1853, but London's system did not reach this stage until 1899.)

In Australia, both Adelaide and Sydney were more advanced than Melbourne in sewerage. Adelaide began constructing a sewerage system in 1878 and Sydney in the 1880s. Hobart followed Melbourne early in the twentieth century.

Brisbane was less advanced than these other capital cities. It is worth giving some details of Brisbane, because this case is probably nearer to the Australian norm. The Queensland government set up a Central Board of Health in 1865—ten years after Victoria—but a Health Act was not passed until 1872. Brisbane Council in 1873 began to discourage cesspits in favour of earth closets, but this campaign was gradual—one block of streets at a time. In 1875 the council began a municipal pan-emptying service but only in certain areas. In the late 1880s, when the pan system was general in Brisbane, some night-soil was stored at depots and some was dumped at sea. The construction of Brisbane's first sewerage project was under way in 1916, but the project ran into technical difficulties and was delayed until 1923.[7] That is, pan closets were still operating in central Brisbane in 1923—and they still operate (along with septic tanks) in many Australian country towns and outer suburbs today. In 1960 it was estimated that half a million people lacked mains sewerage in the Sydney metropolitan area alone.

The transition from the miasmatist to the contagionist approach in public health administration was a godsend for Collingwood. Under the miasmatist regime (see pp. 55–8) Collingwood had suffered greatly, for Collingwood was over-supplied with miasma. To Collingwood's industrialists and councillors, the removal of miasma (at either factory level or municipal level) always seemed discouragingly expensive. The contagionist approach, however, emphasized personal and domestic hygiene: ensuring the purity of milk and food, fumigating an infected house and isolating a patient.

Collingwood was among the first municipalities to buy a lactometer (in 1875) and was one of the few consistently active municipalities in the analysis of milk and food, surpassing even Fitzroy and Melbourne. Collingwood reported analyses to the C.B.H. annually; Melbourne became apathetic after 1885; and Fitzroy's interest dates chiefly from 1890 when eleven households obtaining milk from one dairy there were attacked by typhoid fever. In the 1880s the Collingwood analyst tested about two dozen samples of milk a year. Only about half were pure; about one-quarter were fair or were partially skimmed and (excepting in seasons when milk was over-abundant) one-quarter or more contained from 4 per cent to 44 per cent added water. The offenders were fined. The Collingwood sanitary inspector reported: 'I now have great difficulty in obtaining samples of milk. If I am seen in the streets, drivers of milk carts clear out.'

From 1878 the council also inspected milk-vending premises for hygiene, though with less spectacular results. Collingwood then had about three hundred cattle (two-thirds of them milch cows) but herds were small, often only one or two cows. The cows were kept in backyards, often shut in sheds. They scavenged on garbage, supplemented by cheap hay and by occasional spells in the municipal wasteland along the Merri Creek or in the dwindling vacant allotments. Milk was sold from these backyards and also from various shops, including even small greengrocers. In the early 1890s Collingwood's milk vendors totalled one hundred and were being swollen by the unemployed and the poor. One 'dairy' (said the sanitary inspector) was a four-roomed house containing fourteen people. Other 'dairies' had 'a large number of fowls kept in a very small yard and a setting hen or two in the back verandah and children playing around them, or the drain choked with a bag and a quantity of ducks washing therein'. In the 1890s the council realized belatedly that for years cows had risked infection by drinking diluted sewage in open drains while out grazing or while heading home to be milked. The council finally prohibited the grazing of dairy cattle on any unfenced land, began destroying diseased cattle, and increased the vendor's registration fee from 5s to 20s —level with other municipalities. Thus cow-keeping in Collingwood ceased to be a protected industry.

The sanitary inspector in the 1880s was also busy ordering people to abolish cesspits, to clean and drain their backyards, to fill in stagnant pools in yards or under houses, and to provide proper horse-manure pits. Other entries in the inspector's report book concern: wandering cattle; plumbers digging up roads without permission; butchers boiling down; night-soil dumping; and houses unfit for habitation. And then there was a woman who was reported by the inspector 'for having a dead horse on her premises which she refused to move. It had to be removed by the council's labourers and she was summonsed for expenses which were recovered.'

After 1888 Collingwood and Fitzroy councils were particularly efficient in supervising typhoid fever patients. Infectious cases were removed in an ambulance (instead of in cabs as previously), and the patient's excrement was incinerated in a portable apparatus built conjointly by the two councils. Because tenants were sometimes too poor to buy disinfectants, Collingwood Council took on the responsibility of fumigating infected premises.

The disposal of garbage, street sweepings and dead animals became a growing problem, particularly after 1887 when the Central

Board of Health warned that open refuse-dumps were a health hazard. In 1888 Fitzroy Council, with a twice-weekly collection service, collected two hundred cartloads of garbage and sweepings a week, and buried it in a park in North Fitzroy. In Collingwood, street sweepings were dumped in old brick-holes in Portion 62 and in a gully in Portion 65. It was not until 1890 that Collingwood Council began collecting garbage from premises instead of from streets as formerly. Despite warnings from the C.B.H., Robert Dehnert, the former councillor who wanted to make Collingwood 'a second Manchester' (see p. 105), continued to operate an 'unhealthy' garbage dump in his old brick-hole in Portion 62. His clients were chiefly garbage contractors of Melbourne City Council. According to complaints, new refuse was left uncovered for a day or so; fires sometimes smouldered there, causing air pollution; and Dehnert allowed pigs and milking cows to feed on the refuse. The council unsuccessfully prosecuted Dehnert for five years before securing a conviction and fines in 1893.

From Central Board of Health reports, it is possible to compile the following table showing the official activity of the health inspector in four suburbs for five years to 1890 (aggregate figures):

	C'wood	Fitzroy	North Melb.	South Melb.
Population 1885	25,700	23,400	20,000	31,372
Notices issued	1,033	871	461	311
Persons prosecuted	204	270	74	41
Total fines	£387	£330	£110	£79

Judged accordingly, the health inspectors in both Collingwood and Fitzroy were comparatively busy. The Central Board of Health selected both these councils for praise, along with Prahran and Sandhurst (Bendigo). However, Collingwood Council was a less generous employer than Fitzroy. The inspector's salary in Collingwood was £160 or £175 a year—generally £25 to £30 less than in Fitzroy and other suburbs. Similarly, Collingwood's part-time medical officer of health received £50 a year (the normal fee in major suburbs), but Fitzroy's received £75 a year—the highest in Victoria after Melbourne and Sandhurst. Measured thus, it would seem that, officially, public health supervision was rewarded more highly in Fitzroy than in Collingwood.

During the past hundred years, Melbourne's inner suburbs have been affected enormously by the cycle of economic boom and depression. In particular, the boom of the late 1880s and the depression of the early 1890s hastened the decay of most inner suburbs— and, in many respects, made these suburbs resemble Collingwood.

After reaching a peak of 19,300 in 1866, Collingwood's population dropped slightly—to 18,598 in 1871. It rose again in the 1870s, slowly, to 21,054 in 1875—an increase of less than 2,000 in nine years. By 1881, Collingwood's place as Melbourne's most populous suburb had been taken by Emerald Hill (South Melbourne). During the metropolitan population boom of 1881–91, Collingwood (including the boom area, Clifton Hill) increased by 50 per cent—from 23,829 to 35,070.

Where did Collingwood's population come from and go to? How was it developing in composition? How were living conditions changing?

From the 1860s, some Collingwood men went inland in search of work, either regular or seasonal. The Collingwood *Observer* in 1866 began featuring dispatches from Ballarat and other provincial centres, about opportunities for employment and about the doings of Collingwood men there. Some of these men left wives and children in Collingwood, and visited home when possible. Collingwood's low rents continued to attract widows and deserted wives from other districts. As shown in detail in chapter 2, the number of females for every 100 males in Collingwood rose to a peak of 109 in 1881, making Collingwood the most feminized inner suburb.

Physically, Collingwood was hardly a healthy environment for families. In Collingwood, said the *Observer* in 1875, there are some two thousand two- or three-roomed wooden shanties, in all stages of decay, in which are immured families large enough for houses twice the size . . . With neither comfort, nor convenience, nor quietness at home, the growing lads and girls naturally seek enjoyment elsewhere, and there is a wretched future for the young people thus driven to the streets for recreation.

Thus, as well as retaining its old reputation as an unhealthy place, Collingwood from the 1870s onwards became represented as a sort of modern Sodom and Gomorrah, because of its rowdy larrikins.

Another comment in the *Observer* a decade later, in 1886, suggests a continuing deterioration in the shanties and the type of occupant:

A good fire that would sweep off some acres of the wretched wooden shanties—relics of the early days—would be a blessing to Collingwood, for none but disreputable and improvident people now care to occupy such places, although the best of us would have been glad of them in the early days.

According to the sanitary inspector's report book, the main faults in the worst houses included: stagnant water under floors or in cellars; bad ventilation; uncleanliness; floors resting on earth; lack of water supply; two or three tenements sharing one privy closet. One house was made of palings; 'the ceilings are falling down, the floors are rotten and the walls are blowing about in the wind.' Such houses were attracting 'the lowest vagrants'.

After 1875, especially during epidemics, the council occasionally declared some houses as unfit for habitation—rising to about twenty houses a year during the late 1880s. However, councils in Victoria, unlike those in England, lacked power to enforce demolition. Some houses were demolished voluntarily; others were merely vacated or repaired, and sometimes the occupants even refused to leave.

The absence of parklands or children's playgrounds in Collingwood was not serious (or even particularly noticed) in the 1850s when everybody lived near a vacant, unfenced allotment and within walking distance of the country. But after 1870 the spaces dwindled while the country receded. For example, following the introduction of underground drainage in 1867 and the abolition of the old open 'central drain', several tracts of former swampland (Portions 86, 80 and 67) had their potential changed. Building allotments there were advertised, falsely, as 'high, well drained and respectably situated'. Many of the new houses were financed by building societies which were established in Melbourne and Col-

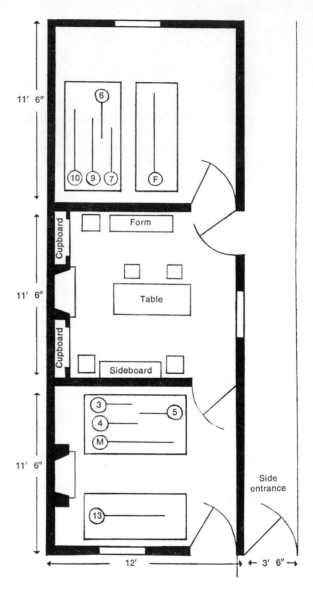

Plan of a three-roomed house in Collingwood, occupied by two adults and eight children, 1937. Figures in circles indicate children's ages.

lingwood from the mid-1860s. The societies offered 'facilities by which the worst-paid working-man may obtain a roof of his own over his head, merely by paying, for a few years, an ordinary rent'.

The increasing squeeze may be seen clearly in Portion 67. When speculator John Hodgson sold Portion 67 and neighbouring lands in 1841, his ground-plan provided for spacious semi-rural allotments with depths of 115 ft and frontages of 91 ft. Until 1867, about half (say, ten acres) of Portion 67 was kept useless by the central drain. There was even uncertainty about who owned the land. The other half was dotted with horses, cows, poultry and about two dozen scattered shacks. In 1868 a section of the council sought to acquire the newly drained ten acres as a recreation reserve for the already populated surrounding portions. However, underground drainage altered the potential and value of the ten acres, and by 1873 the land had passed into the hands of the highest bidder, the Metropolitan Building Society. The land became advertised as: 'valuable freehold building allotments. The working classes should avail themselves of the present opportunity. The terms are one-fifth cash [and the balance over eight years].' The building society, seeking maximum profits, revised Hodgson's ground-plan, reducing the depths to 63 ft and the frontages to 25 ft, thereby managing to squeeze in two streets more than Hodgson had and creating many more frontages. As the streets (with one exception) were designed to facilitate 'through' traffic, much land was tied up in traffic purposes and much money was consumed in road construction. An alternative would have been to use some of that space and finance in pedestrian squares and an internal play area, but this idea was foreign to the commercial grid-layout. By the end of the 1880s, the would-be parkland in Portion 67 was covered with about 180 cottages (chiefly single-storey, detached, wooden), with perhaps 800 inhabitants—including several hundred children who now had to play on the street.

In Collingwood, even newly built houses were usually of low quality by metropolitan standards. In southern Fitzroy, there had always been building regulations that discouraged small or wooden houses. Collingwood Council adopted its first building regulations only in 1874, and these were perfunctory and inadequate; Collingwood had no 'brick area' and there was, for example, no minimum size for rooms. Furthermore, the regulations were not strictly enforced, as the council was afraid of diverting potential population and revenue to other suburbs.

After a subdivision at 130 Islington Street (Portion 67) in the

1870s, a house was built 8 ft 6 in. wide. Beside the house is a public lane which is 2 ft 6 in. wider than the house—a significant comment on living conditions in Collingwood.

During the land boom of the 1880s, the *Observer* noticed a movement of 'better-off folk' away from Collingwood:

> A great drawback . . . in Collingwood is the want of suitable . . . dwelling-houses for the better class of the industrial community . . . Consequently when Collingwood folk get a little up in the world, or when young Collingwoodians get married, they migrate to the comfortable and respectable cottages erected by enterprising capitalists in North Fitzroy.

This exodus was probably a symptom of, as well as a contributing factor in, the deteriorating situation.

Some aspects of this demographic process are illustrated by the career of George David Langridge. A carpenter from Kent, Langridge arrived about 1852, aged twenty-three. Disappointed on the goldfields, he settled in a primitive shack on Collingwood Flat and gradually developed from 'carpenter' to 'general contractor'. In 1866 he opened an estate agency in Collingwood and was sometimes described as an 'architect'. He was a Collingwood councillor for nine years after 1865, being mayor twice. He entered parliament for Collingwood in 1874, and was continually returned, becoming Victoria's Chief Secretary in the 1880s. Langridge was a prominent promoter of Collingwood building societies, thus helping many people, including himself, to improve their address. In 1864 he was living in a small brick cottage in narrow, muddy Harmsworth Street (Portion 74), with a net annual value of only £24. By 1870 he had moved up to Clifton Hill, near a reserve called the Mayor's Park. In 1883 he built a mansion for himself on a large allotment at 12 North Terrace, Clifton Hill, opposite the Darling Gardens; his net annual value there was £156 in 1885 and £250 in 1888. The highly successful Langridge Mutual Permanent Building Society, which he founded in 1880, soon moved its headquarters from Collingwood to the city and had dealings throughout the metropolitan area. He also developed other business interests. Thus the carpenter from the Flat became the statesman and financier of Clifton Hill.

Meanwhile the inner suburbs received some poor people from the City of Melbourne. In the five years 1886–90, 668 houses in the City of Melbourne were condemned by the City Council and vacated. Of these, about 30 per cent were promptly demolished,

View from the tower of Collingwood Town Hall, 1885, looking westward across Portion 67 towards Fitzroy, with the Exhibition Building in Carlton on the horizon. In the foreground are Collingwood shacks from the gold era—and market gardens.

View from the tower of Collingwood Town Hall, 1955, looking in the same direction as the previous picture. Most of the shacks shown in the earlier picture have been replaced by factories.

about 32 per cent were repaired and re-occupied, and 38 per cent remained vacant while their fate was being decided. In addition, many city landlords demolished voluntarily. The new buildings tended to be shops, warehouses and other commercial concerns. There was no public provision of alternative accommodation for the poorer persons thus displaced. They had to herd more together, or seek cheap houses in the nearer suburbs. As well as increasing Collingwood's poor, this process contributed to the 'proletariani-zation' of Carlton and Fitzroy.

To exploit the demand for cheap housing, Collingwood builders after 1880 specialized in rows of attached houses, with party walls. A builder might demolish two adjoining, unattached shacks and replace them with an attached row of four. A typical Collingwood row would be six single-storey houses on a 96 ft frontage—i.e. 16 ft each—with backyards of 16 ft by 20 ft. In one case a corner allot-ment, measuring 85 ft by 125 ft, with three frontages, was used to build twelve two-storey houses, each with a backyard measuring 15 ft by 9 ft. In the early twentieth century, this row was owned by Labor Party federal parliamentarian King O'Malley. Colling-wood row-houses were rarely comparable with the charming ter-races of other suburbs. For one thing, under Collingwood's lax building controls, row-houses could be made chiefly of wood, with brick being required only for the party walls.

Among Melbourne's biggest jerry-builders of the 1880s were the Slater brothers—Benjamin (plasterer) and Daniel (bricklayer). Born in Manchester, they settled in Collingwood in the early 1880s and in three years they erected 110 dwellings (sometimes in rows of up to ten) in Collingwood, Fitzroy and Flemington. When Benjamin unsuccessfully stood for Collingwood Council in 1887, he was a large ratepayer, with dozens of houses in course of erection, and he claimed to have 'perhaps a larger stake in Darling Ward than any other citizen'. In some Slater houses the drainpipes from the backyard discharged not into the back lane but into a stagnant pool under the house, and by 1889 the Collingwood inspector reported these houses as unfit for habitation.

Predictably, most of Collingwood's worst houses were owned by absentee landlords. If we analyse the 53 houses reported by the sanitary inspector in 1886 and 1887 as being unfit for habitation, we find that 5 houses (or 9 per cent) were occupied by the owners and 48 (or 91 per cent) by tenants. Where did the landlords live? If we analyse 71 tenanted dwellings complained of by the inspector (for various sanitary misdemeanours) in 1892–7 (inclusive), we find that only 34 per cent of these owners lived in Collingwood (often next door to the unsatisfactory house); 20 per cent lived in Fitzroy; and 46 per cent lived in other districts. Some of the landlords owned whole rows of houses.

To the embarrassment of Collingwood's landlords and councillors, statements continually appeared in the Melbourne press about poverty and slums in Collingwood. For example, in 1891 the Reverend Dr Charles Strong, of the Australian Church, gave evidence about Collingwood slums to a Royal Commission on Charities, receiving a wide press coverage. The Collingwood *Observer* denounced Dr Strong's evidence, and the press elaboration, as grossly exaggerated: 'We [the *Observer*] certainly came across what may be called rookeries . . . but they were of a very mild nature—at the outside, five weatherboard cottages facing a common yard—yet all dry and well drained.' Evidently the *Observer* was putting the view of property-owners. The Melbourne *Herald* noted that Collingwood property-owners 'nurse a hostile feeling towards Dr Strong. They are averse to having any light thrown on the condition of their properties.'[1]

The general trend in Collingwood housing can be traced in census figures. Between 1861 and 1891 there was a gradual increase in numbers of larger houses and brick houses (particularly in Clifton Hill), and a gradual decline in numbers of one- and two-roomed wooden shacks. Even so, the typical Collingwood house in 1881 was still wooden and was still the smallest in the metropolis, with only 3.87 rooms, compared with 4.71 (probably brick) in Fitzroy (about the average for the metropolis) and 6.61 in St Kilda (the highest). And Collingwood's rooms were among the most crowded (1.21 persons per room in 1881, surpassed only by Hotham and Footscray). In Fitzroy, on the other hand, the numbers of people and rooms were almost level in 1881, and in 1891 Fitzroy as a whole (and three of its five wards, particularly the two wards in North Fitzroy) achieved the status of having more rooms than people—a status previously enjoyed (in 1881) by only four suburbs (Prahran, St Kilda, Brighton, Hawthorn). In 1891 only one of Collingwood's five wards (Loch Ward in Clifton Hall) had more rooms than people.

Another way to compare residential densities is to examine the Board of Works sewerage plans of 1897, showing all buildings in various suburbs. If we calculate the number of houses per acre in sample parts of old Collingwood (south of Reilly Street), we find that it ranges from 11.4 houses per acre to 17.6 houses per acre, with

15.1 houses per acre being typical of most areas. In Clifton Hill, however, we find densities of only 7.8 houses per acre and even 6.4 houses per acre.

The 'public image' of Collingwood and Fitzroy is seen in lavish guide books about Australia published in the 1880s. One book, *Victoria and Its Metropolis*, noted that Collingwood's population 'was mostly employed in the [local] factories', while Fitzroy was 'much less given over to factories'. 'Its [Fitzroy's] streets are mostly two-storeyed dwellings in constant rows; these are the homes of people engaged in the city who wish to dwell within easy walking distance from their avocations.' Another book, *Cassell's Picturesque Australasia*, said: 'The different suburbs have characters of their own. The working-men are most at home in Collingwood, Prahran and Hotham . . . Carlton and Fitzroy may be described as middle-class or bourgeois suburbs.'

Having surveyed Collingwood's developing private space—its habitations and inhabitants—we turn now to its developing public space—its streets and transport.

This involves an examination of council affairs. In some ways the Collingwood Council of the 1870s and 1880s was different from that of the 1850s and 1860s, described in chapters 3 and 4. An analysis of the sixty-seven councillors between 1855 and 1881 shows that, taking the period as a whole, the average age of incoming councillors was 41.8 years and the average length of service was 4.0 years. However, if the 27-year period is divided into three shorter periods, an interesting difference appears:

	1855–63	*1864–72*	*1873–81*
Average age of new councillors	39·6 years	40·0 years	48·0 years
Average length of service in council	2·8 years	4·3 years	5·6 years

This is largely a reflection of the fact that the energetic young gold immigrants who made their impact on Victoria in the 1850s were now growing old. In the 1850s and 1860s, council seats were widely contested, with up to nine candidates for three vacancies, but after 1871 the field narrowed and it became usual for one or two of the three retiring councillors (or the whole three in 1878) to be returned unopposed for longer terms—up to twelve or fifteen years. By 1881, then, Collingwood councillors were approximating the common stereotype of municipal 'old fogies'.

Some things, however, changed little. Council politics continued to be largely about geographical rivalries, as described in chapters

3 and 4—an interest up here pitted against an interest down there. Even after the division of the municipality into three wards in 1864, tensions existed not only between one ward and another, but also between parts of a ward. This was particularly so in Victoria Ward, which was the largest ward, occupying more than half the municipality (between Hoddle Street and the Yarra). Victoria Ward ratepayers split into four distinct interest-groups, each based on a particular street; these four streets competed for the three Victoria Ward positions on the council.

In order to improve the riverside manufacturing area, interested persons advocated the building of a bridge at the end of Simpson's Road (Victoria Street) to connect with Barker's Road, Kew. As a result of such a bridge, said the *Observer* in 1865, 'four miles of a main road frontage would be gained, and shanties would make room for villas'. The campaign for a bridge continued for two decades. In 1870 a Great Victoria Bridge Committee, comprising Simpson's Road property holders, made representations to the government. Brickmaker Robert Dehnert, of Portion 62, entered the council in 1874 in order (he said) to seek for Victoria Street a bridge and more factories. In 1880, after tolls had been abolished in Victoria, the directors of the privately owned Studley Park bridge decided to dismantle that bridge. Victoria Street residents feared that, unless the proposed Victoria Street bridge was built soon, business would be drained away northwards to Johnston Street. The Victoria Street bridge was finally built in 1882. Woolwasher Peter Nettleton donated a piece of land, and soap and candle manufacturer Henry Walker subscribed £100.

In the 1870s, property owners in the south-west (Barkly Ward) tried to persuade the council to buy up property in Portion 52 in order to connect Langridge Street with Fitzroy's Gertrude Street. A Langridge Street publican entered the council in 1881 and helped to bring about the extension in 1882. Presumably he and his electors benefited from the increased traffic.

In the mid-1870s the structure of Victorian local government was amended, giving municipalities wide borrowing powers and giving the most highly developed municipalities (including Collingwood in 1876 and Fitzroy in 1878) the title of 'city' instead of 'town'. Henceforth municipal political argument was increasingly about whether, and how much, money ought to be borrowed and whether it ought to be spent on essentials such as street works or on luxuries such as a town hall.

About 1880 Collingwood Council was deeply split over a majority decision to borrow £40,000 for public works, including a town hall surpassing Fitzroy's. The loan was opposed by Smith Street businessmen and (inside the council) by the three councillors of Darling Ward; this ward included the bulk of the Smith Street shopping centre, as well as much of Clifton Hill. These councillors argued that the loan would involve imposing a special rate (in addition to the existing general rate) to cover loan repayments and that this was taxing the rising generation for the benefit of the present one. By raising technical objections and leaving the council without a quorum, the minority managed to delay the loan for two years, while the majority retaliated by thwarting business relating to Darling Ward.

In 1883 the council held a referendum, resulting in an overwhelming vote in favour of the loan. This was probably because the loan was for street works as well as for a town hall. The few votes against were said to be chiefly from Smith Street businessmen.

The Darling Ward councillors then resolved to see that the loan was spent to Darling Ward's advantage. For example, since it was universally assumed that a new town hall would increase the value of its immediate locality, they opposed (unsuccessfully) the site chosen for the town hall in Victoria Ward (in Portion 66, formerly a swamp, in Hoddle Street), contending that the intersection of Hoddle and Johnston Streets (further north, in Darling Ward) was a 'more important line of traffic'.

Of the £40,000 loan, £28,000 was allocated to street works and drainage and £12,000 to the town hall. The hall, costing £30,000, was financed partly from other sources, including a government grant and the sale of Collingwood's old municipal sites. Thus yet another suburb built its lavish status symbol, while the metropolis continued to lack sewerage.

Among people who were active in municipal politics, the building of suburban town halls was welcomed as a boost to the building industry. For example, among those associated with the Collingwood town hall project was William McBurnie, a builder who had been a Collingwood resident and radical political activist since the 1850s. He entered Collingwood Council in 1879, and resigned from it in 1883 in order to become overseer at a new quarry which the council was establishing. As quarry overseer, he maintained contact with councillors. In 1884 he helped to campaign for the return of Councillor Michael Dwyer, an influential councillor who was currently mayor. In 1885 ex-Councillor McBurnie was appointed as clerk of works for the construction of the town hall.

At least two other Collingwood councillors were involved in suburban town hall construction. In 1885 Councillor William Smith and his building partner (a former Collingwood councillor) shared a contract for a town hall at Caulfield, a southern suburb. In 1887, as we noted in chapter 8, Councillor Smith opposed plans for a Melbourne and Metropolitan Board of Works.

Similar conflicts occurred over proposals to introduce tramways and railways in Collingwood and Fitzroy. We shall consider tramways first.

In the 1850s, public transport in Melbourne streets consisted of the old-established one-horse cabs and the new multi-horse omnibuses. About 1860 a new experiment was being conducted in London—horse-drawn trams. In Sydney a horse-drawn tram began to run in Pitt Street in 1861, between the harbour ferry terminal and the railway terminal. From 1860, several companies were interested in establishing horse or steam trams in Melbourne. One proposed route was from Melbourne to Clifton Hill, via Gertrude Street and Smith Street. In 1862 the proposal was supported briefly by Fitzroy Council, but was vehemently opposed by various interests in both municipalities. The objectors held a public meeting, enlisted the aid of the three local parliamentarians and organized a petition with eight hundred signatures.

The case against trams throughout the 1860s, as reported in the *Observer*, was that they would damage the local economy. Freelance cabmen and draymen, it said, would be displaced by an anonymous corporate monopoly; local blacksmiths, coachbuilders and saddlers would lose business because the tram company would be controlled from outside the district; even if horses were used instead of steam, the tram company would be unlikely to patronize local hay and corn merchants; suburban shopping streets were too narrow to take on a new function; if the poor road surfaces required trams to run close to the kerb, this would interfere with shopkeepers' and customers' vehicles standing at the kerbside; if the rail was kept down to the level of the broken metal, the metal would enter the groove and de-rail the tram; if the rail was raised as in orthodox railways, existing traffic (i.e., customers) would be repelled; if steam was used, this would frighten horses and pollute the shops with smoke and noise; anyway, trams would not bring customers to Collingwood and Fitzroy but would siphon away local residents to the city shops.

For similar reasons, the advent of trams was resisted also in London, Sydney and other cities. In Sydney, for example, the Pitt Street service was discontinued after five years.

However, developments in the 1870s modified the anti-tram case somewhat. Asphalt made it possible for tram tracks to be embedded and to be in the centre of the road. Tram companies in Melbourne envisaged trams that were lighter, more comfortable, less cumbersome and less noisy than before. A steam tramway, with double-deck cars, was established in Sydney in 1879. It survived controversy and, by 1885, Sydney had more than 27 miles of tramway.

Trams became a lively issue in Melbourne about 1880. The Victorian Tramway Company and the Melbourne Tramway and Omnibus Company were lobbying among parliamentarians and among municipal councillors, seeking permission to begin constructing tracks in the streets. As Melbourne town clerk E. G. Fitz-Gibbon recalled later, the M.T.O. Company 'secured the election of members to the council, and obtained the support of several already there'. One of the fourteen directors who introduced the Victorian Tramway Company was Councillor Henry Walker, mayor of Collingwood in 1880–1. Interestingly, Walker was also a pioneer of asphalt paving.

In a ballot of ratepayers conducted by Collingwood Council in 1881, the 1,063 ratepayers who participated were almost evenly divided about the introduction of tramways, with a majority of 13 against. The opponents of trams were more vocal than the supporters. At an anti-tram rally in Fitzroy in 1881, fears were expressed for the future of retailers such as produce dealers, and tradesmen such as coachbuilders, as well as cabmen. However, many opponents of trams obviously had nothing directly personal at stake and merely regarded trams as 'bad for the district'.

In Collingwood, the feeling against trams was significantly stronger inside the council (six votes to three) than outside. The pro-tram councillors in 1882 comprised a manufacturer, a publican and a building contractor. One of these councillors said that he accepted trams as inevitable, provided that the inhabitants of the streets concerned agreed and provided that steam motors were not used. (In 1882 the tramway promoters agreed to use either horses or, if possible, underground cables instead of steam.) The anti-tram councillors included only one with any apparent direct interest (a produce dealer); the other five comprised a master cooper, a

builder, a maltster, a property-owner and a city clothing manufacturer.

In some cases, anti-tram attitudes were linked with a generally
conservative personal outlook. Councillor Andrew Wright (property-owner) was described by the *Observer* as 'a rigid old Tory'
who was opposed to tramways, municipal loans 'and such-like
inventions of democracy'. Another prominent opponent of trams
in 1881–2 was Thomas Upton, a building contractor, who had
been a Collingwood councillor in the 1870s. In 1892 Upton stood
(unsuccessfully) for parliament with conservative views—opposed
to the Trades Hall, opposed to the payment of parliamentarians,
opposed to the principle of one-man-one-vote.

In the mid-1880s one of the main arguments against trams—that
they would take shoppers away from Collingwood and bring none
to it—withered away. The land boom created a new outer fringe of
suburbia beyond Collingwood—in Clifton Hill, North Fitzroy and
Northcote. Traders in Smith Street and Brunswick Street came to
realize that, with trams, they were better placed than their Melbourne competitors to tap this new market. Fitzroy Council, which
was more partial towards Brunswick Street than to the Fitzroy
side of Smith Street, even tried (unsuccessfully) to have the proposed
routes altered so that trams from Clifton Hill, as well as the one
from North Fitzroy, would pass through Brunswick Street, not
Smith Street. Similarly, Victoria Street (Simpson's Road) which
had previously been a stronghold of anti-tram feeling, had its
potential altered in 1884 by the opening of the new bridge over
the Yarra connecting with Barker's Road, Kew, and the boom
suburbs of Hawthorn and Camberwell. When cable trams began
running in Melbourne from 1885, Collingwood and Fitzroy were
on the road to more places than ever before.

In the 1860s, when there were already railways from Flinders
Street, Melbourne, to an eastern suburb (Hawthorn) and to southern suburbs (St Kilda, Prahran and Brighton), the question arose
of whether the northern suburbs should share in any future railways development. In particular, if a Gippsland–Melbourne railway was built, should it enter the city via the existing Prahran–
Brighton line or through the northern suburbs? In 1867 the
northern route was advocated by an Upper Yarra Railway League,
based at Heidelberg. The league held public meetings in Heidelberg and Collingwood, and proposed a route embracing Melbourne, Carlton, Fitzroy, Collingwood, Northcote, Heidelberg,

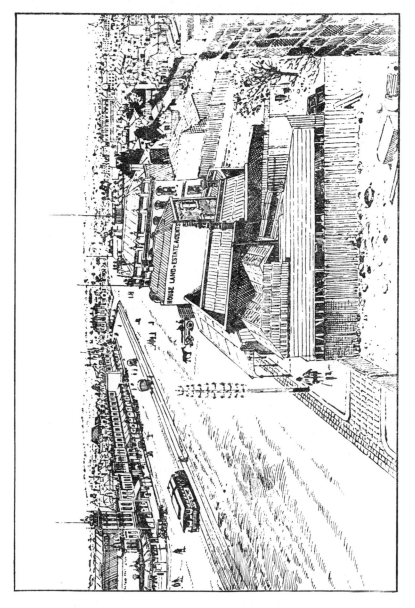

Queen's Parade, Clifton Hill, 1891, looking towards Northcote and Heidelberg.

Lilydale and Gippsland. A northern route (called an 'outer circle') was again urged in the 1870s when the Gippsland line was built.

In the 1870s Fitzroy and Collingwood were interested less in the convenience of a train service than in economic benefits resulting from the hustle and bustle of the metropolitan terminal. If the Gippsland line went (as it eventually did) through the municipality of Prahran, the metropolitan terminal would be in Flinders Street, far from Fitzroy-Collingwood; but if the Gippsland railway went through the northern suburbs, the terminal could be near, or even in, Fitzroy-Collingwood. The terminal sites envisaged by the northern interests were (in 1867) Nicholson Street, Fitzroy, and (in 1874) the city site occupied today by the Royal Melbourne Institute of Technology. This proximity, it was thought, would have boosted Fitzroy-Collingwood land values, population and trade. Many people, ranging from Fitzroy shopkeepers to Collingwood cabmen, expected to benefit. However, by the late 1870s, Melbourne's Spencer Street and Flinders Street stations had been confirmed as the two metropolitan terminals.

The pro-railway forces in the northern suburbs campaigned jointly until about 1880. Then fragmentation developed. Heidelberg remained fairly satisfied with an outer circle route skirting around Clifton Hill, North Fitzroy, North Carlton and Royal Park to the Spencer Street terminal. But this, it was realized, would be of little convenience to Collingwood and Fitzroy people, who now began advocating a shorter, direct Heidelberg–Melbourne route through either Collingwood or Fitzroy to the Flinders Street terminal. Henceforth the pro-railway forces in Collingwood and Fitzroy campaigned against each other. And within each of these two suburbs, agitation for or against railways arose from groups who expected that a direct route would affect—favourably or unfavourably—their particular street or occupation.

When in 1880 the government proposed a direct Heidelberg–Melbourne route through Collingwood-Richmond Flat, the scheme received support in Collingwood on grounds that it would result in much government money being spent in Collingwood on labour and that it would economically improve the Flat. However, because of the benefit to the Flat, the scheme was opposed by some Smith Street interests who feared a shift of balance.

In 1881 a prominent Fitzroy citizen recommended that the Heidelberg–Melbourne railway should run through a tunnel along the length of Napier Street, Fitzroy, with a grand Fitzroy station at Smith's Swamp on Portion 85. This scheme, however, was expected to alienate Fitzroy's Brunswick Street merchants, who, the local press said, 'object to any new means of transit which would take their customers to Melbourne and interfere with their trade monopoly'. The government preferred any direct route to be through Collingwood, not Fitzroy. Henceforth, suggestions for a Fitzroy railway station often involved a short spur line annexed to the main Collingwood route. One spur briefly considered was along Reilly Street, from the Collingwood line to Smith's Swamp, Fitzroy; Collingwood Council hoped vainly that the government would therefore take over the Reilly Street drain.

In 1882 the Collingwood direct route met difficulties. The cost of buying land on the Collingwood-Richmond Flat was found to be discouraging; and Richmond Council objected that the railway would cut Richmond in half and interfere with drainage lines. The Collingwood direct route was provided for in the Railway Act 1886, but construction was delayed, partly because of agitation from Fitzroy. In both suburbs, rival railway leagues were formed, with numerous public meetings. Eventually, the government pleaded lack of finance, and postponed the project. When Melbourne and Heidelberg were linked by rail in 1888, it was by the outer circle route from Spencer Street through Royal Park and North Carlton. Two short spur lines—to Collingwood (Victoria Park station in Portion 78) and Fitzroy (in the Edinburgh Gardens) —were added, but were of little convenience to Collingwood or Fitzroy. Collingwood and Fitzroy continued to compete in the 1890s for a direct link to Flinders Street. Collingwood won, but not until 1901.

Collingwood and Fitzroy received relatively little benefit from the boom in tramways and railways. One consequence was that middle-class or white-collar people working in the city or in Smith Street could leave their Fitzroy homes and move out to more attractive dormitory areas. The less affluent stayed in Fitzroy, making the average economic condition of Fitzroy more like that of Collingwood.

The boom of the 1880s in land, railways and tramways resulted in the disappearance of Collingwood's few remaining paddocks. One was the 86-acre Dight's Paddock (Portions 78, 79, 88) which had been bought from the Crown for £1,173 in 1838 and sold by the Dight family for £21,000 in 1878, still covered with gum trees. The subdivider was Edwin Trenerry, who had migrated from Cornwall to Ballarat in the mid-1850s, aged eighteen; in the 1860s he became a large shareholder in a deep-shaft mining company. The paddock was auctioned in 1881 as 262 building allotments (complete with a 'proposed railway' which was delayed until 1888). Collingwood Council paid £250 an acre for a recreation reserve which became enclosed as a league football ground.

Another big subdivision of the 1880s was the mansion and garden of wool-dealer Jesse Fairchild (occupying the western half of Portion 60), which in 1885 was bought by a syndicate headed by Thomas Bent, M.L.A., and was subdivided into 150 building allotments. The syndicate's advertisements stressed that land values in the district would be increased by the proposed new Collingwood town hall, by the proposed Richmond–Collingwood railway and by the proposed cable tramway proceeding along Victoria Street to the recently opened Victoria Street bridge linking Collingwood more directly with Kew and Hawthorn. The mansion was preserved temporarily, but the garden was obliterated. In the twentieth century the site is dominated by the Abbotsford Brewery of Carlton and United Breweries Ltd.

It is fitting to end this chapter with a look at Collingwood's continuing industrial development.

In addition to the traditional noxious trades (surveyed in chapters 6 and 7), other industries developed from the mid-1860s onwards. There was a steam-powered sawmill in Smith Street, another in Fitzroy and another in East Melbourne—each employing up to thirty men and boys, as well as providing work for carriers. In 1867 a flax mill was established in Portion 65, on the former swamp where Collingwood's newly constructed underground drain emptied into the Yarra. The mill had a large wheel, driven by water in the drain. The mill immediately began employing 'a considerable number of hands: men, women and children'.

Other Collingwood industries mentioned in council minutes or press advertisements in the late 1860s include a manufacturer of ovens, a coach and buggy builder, and a jam factory. A cigar manufacturer in Cambridge Street was employing twelve hands in 1881. A bluestone building beside the Yarra in Portion 88 (operating as Dight's flour mill until the late 1850s, when it was damaged by a financial collapse and by a flood) was used by a succession of manufacturers after 1870—first as a paper factory, then as a blasting-powder factory and (after 1888) as the Yarra Falls Roller Flour Mills.

The industrialists of the 1870s received much encouragement from a pillar of the Collingwood community named Joel Eade. The son of a Cornish farmer, Eade learned carpentry and joinery before migrating to Victoria, via California, in the 1850s. After goldfields experience, he settled in Collingwood in 1862 as a building contractor and 'architect'. He was mayor of Collingwood in 1870, and became a committee member of the Chamber of Manfactures. An Anglican, he was an energetic supporter or initiator of efforts to 'improve' the community both industrially and morally—a colonial Samuel Smiles. To enable young working men to attend part-time classes in 'useful' subjects, he founded in 1871 the Collingwood School of Design and Artisans' School of Practical Works—a colonial counterpart of English 'steam intellect societies' and the forerunner of Victoria's technical schools. In addition to practical lessons, the youths were told 'how they should act with respect to their masters, and that they should strive in some measure to repay the gentlemen who were taking so much trouble to advance their future welfare'.

However, such sentiments do not typify the commercial-industrial system of Collingwood. When a policeman went to the Collingwood Boot Factory at the Glasshouse in 1867 to arrest a young worker over a recent street fight, workers followed the policeman from the factory and allegedly assaulted him; and the Collingwood *Manufacturer* commented:

> We are sorry to see that a factory employing so many hands is not under better discipline, for surely the managers could prevent such disgraceful disorder . . . We hope our much prized factories are not to be turned into schools of demoralization, where the law cannot be executived [*sic*] but at the peril of the officer's life.[2]

A century later, newspapers were publishing similar editorials about universities.

Government statistics on production show that factories grew in size and number in the 1870s and 1880s in both Fitzroy and Collingwood, especially in the latter. These statistics cover all factories, excepting breweries and brickyards. In 1871 Fitzroy and Collingwood each had 36 factories; by 1893 Fitzroy had increased to 71 and Collingwood to 120. The increase in horsepower over that period is significant: a four-fold increase in Fitzroy (to 437) and a ten-fold increase in Collingwood (to 1,170). The inclusion of breweries would enormously boost the figures for Collingwood. (In 1970, Collingwood had about 700 factories, ranging from one-room workshops to large mills.)

Since the 1860s, Collingwood-Fitzroy has been noted as the major centre of footwear manufacturing in Victoria. This was because Collingwood was convenient to the tanneries, convenient to the retail stores in the City of Melbourne and in Smith Street and Brunswick Street, and because it had plentiful supplies of labour. In the 1860s, locally made footwear was produced on a small scale at shoe shops—usually for a particular customer. Gradually a primitive factory system developed, with some of the work being done at four or five large Collingwood shoe factories and some being contracted to freelance bootmakers. In the 1860s some machinery was introduced. The industry benefited from a series of protective tariffs after 1866, and from the doubling of Victoria's population between 1861 and 1891. Together, Collingwood and Fitzroy accounted for 21 per cent of Melbourne's footwear establishments in 1861, 50 per cent in 1891, 47 per cent in 1911, 71 per cent in 1938 and 47 per cent in 1965.[3]

By the 1880s, Collingwood was also becoming an important centre for textiles, with two hat factories and a clothing factory. The hat industry makes an interesting case study. In 1874 Councillor James Hobson Turner, the tannery proprietor who figures in chapter 7, joined with a partner in establishing the Denton Hat Mill in Nicholson Street, Portion 58, opposite the Turner tannery. It was claimed as the first steam-powered hat factory in Australia. Its two storeys and chimney stack dominated the skyline, symbolizing the future Collingwood. The air pollution for which Councillor Turner was already responsible (tannery smells) took on a new, significant form—smoke. Residents again complained to the council unsuccessfully. The factory was a logical development from Collingwood's earlier skin-washing and tanning industries, for the raw materials used (wool, or rabbits' fur, or leather) were cleaned and treated on the premises. Business, initially slack while the public was being weaned from imported hats, improved after 1876 under a new manager-lessee, Thomas Shelmerdine, son of a Lancashire hat-manufacturer. Employees (half of them women and girls doing, *inter alia*, ornamental work) rose from 12 in 1874 to 70 in 1876, 120 in 1883 and 208 in 1887. Turnover reached £30,000 a year.

In 1882 Shelmerdine left the Denton mill to build Collingwood's second hat factory—in the newly subdivided Portion 88 (Dight's Paddock). Near where the Dight family had operated a water-mill, he installed a 20-horsepower gas engine, said to be unique in Victoria, and in five years increased his hands from 50 to 110. Water pumped from the Yarra was dumped into it after use.

Shelmerdine represents an intermediate stage in Collingwood's pastoral–industrial continuum. The Shelmerdine family lived in the old Dight homestead (Yarra House) adjoining the factory (closer to the factory, therefore, than any of their employees were), and, although they mixed primarily with business and professional people and sent their children away to private schools elsewhere, they were identified with Collingwood. After Shelmerdine died in 1898, the factory was acquired first by a businessman who lived in the southern suburbs and later by a hat manufacturers' amalgamation—i.e., a transition from tangible local entrepreneur, to absentee entrepreneur, to anonymous absentee corporation. After World War I, the remaining Shelmerdines moved from Yarra House to the eastern suburbs, and the house was displaced by yet more factory buildings, now owned by the Dunlop international rubber organization.

A similar trend can be seen in the brewing industry. Breweries thrived in the 1880s. Although they decreased in number, they increased enormously in size and output. Apart from the Victoria Brewery (on the Melbourne side of the Melbourne-Collingwood boundary), Collingwood in 1871 had five breweries with 83 employees, compared with Fitzroy's two breweries with 19 employees; in 1893 Collingwood had four breweries with 157 employees, and Fitzroy had none. Collingwood's four breweries included three old-established ones (the Yorkshire in Wellington Street, the Burton in Cambridge Street and the Shamrock in Victoria Street—all mentioned in chapter 6) and a new one (Foster's in Rokeby Street). Collingwood in 1891 was Victoria's biggest brewing centre outside the City of Melbourne. In the 1880s, control of the breweries passed from the original master brewers to companies, private companies first, then public ones, with the Collingwood interests shrinking in significance. Thus Collingwood drinkers became less likely to be personally acquainted with the manufacturers of their beer.

The Yorkshire Brewery is a good example of this process. We have seen in chapter 6 how publican John Wood began the Yorkshire as a one-man, backyard enterprise. In the 1880s, after he had extensively enlarged the Yorkshire, Wood lived in a mansion—not in Collingwood, but across the Yarra in non-industrial Hawthorn. After he died in 1883, the Yorkshire was carried on by his sons. In 1887 it was taken over and formed into a company. One of the company's directors, Godwin George Crespin, further illustrates our point. As a young man, Crespin lived in Collingwood Flat, and at twenty-six he entered Collingwood Council. At thirty-six he became a partner in an auctioneering firm, which eventually became Australia's largest sugar-broking firm. With these successes, Crespin moved from Collingwood to Kew, and entered Kew Council and Melbourne City Council.

By the 1880s, the Shamrock Brewery in Portion 62 had passed from the hands of the original proprietor, Thomas Graham, to a partnership, Boyd and Head, who closed their existing Fitzroy brewery and considerably enlarged the Shamrock at Collingwood. In 1888 the Shamrock was taken over by a public company.

The Foster Lager Brewery in Rokeby Street was built in 1888 by two Americans, W. M. and R. Foster. It became a private company the following year, and almost gained a monopoly of Melbourne's bottled beer trade.

The story is similar at Thomas Aitken's Victoria Brewery. As a sign of the growing complexity of the brewing industry, the Victoria in the 1880s was equipped throughout with a network of bells for internal communication, as well as being linked by telephone with the City and with Aitken's distillery in Northumberland Street, Collingwood (Portion 53). After Aitken died in 1884, the Victoria changed hands and in 1888 became a public company.

Breweries were badly affected by the depression of the 1890s. This accelerated a tendency for breweries to merge with, or absorb, each other. One by one, the Collingwood breweries became connected with the Carlton Brewery Limited, of Bouverie Street, Carlton.

First to go were the Yorkshire and Burton breweries. By 1899, both these had ceased production, and had handed over their trade to the Carlton Brewery Limited. The Burton remained closed, but the Carlton began renting the premises of the Yorkshire.

The Victoria Brewing, Malting and Distilling Company Limited was in financial trouble by 1894, and was taken over by London investors. In 1904 it was in trouble again, and was taken over by the Carlton.

The Shamrock Brewing Company Limited and the Foster Brewing Company Proprietary Limited survived the depression, but in 1907 they amalgamated with the Carlton Brewery Limited (and with two other metropolitan brewing companies) to form Carlton and United Breweries Proprietary Limited, which became a public company in 1913. In 1909 Carlton and United absorbed the Melbourne Co-operative Brewery Company Limited which was estab-

Aerial view of the Housing Commission estate in Portion 74, Collingwood, looking westward from Hoddle Street.

Model of Housing Commission row-houses, Clifton Hill.

A string of identical detached wooden houses in Rupert Street, Collingwood (Portion 67), built in the 1870s by a building society.

A house 8 feet 6 inches wide at 130 Islington Street, Collingwood.

lished in 1904 and which operated the Abbotsford Brewery, in Church Street (Portion 60).

Today the enormous production of Carlton and United is concentrated at three brewing plants—the Carlton, the Victoria and the Abbotsford. These are the only three plants surviving from the dozen or so that have been absorbed into the Carlton empire since 1894.

Apart from Carlton and United Breweries Limited, scores of large companies (and hundreds of small ones) have a stake in Collingwood today. Whereas this book has been concerned chiefly with individual entrepreneurs, the historian of twentieth-century Collingwood will be concerned, *inter alia*, with corporate names such as the Phoenix Biscuit Company Proprietary Limited, the Saxone Shoe Company Australia Proprietary Limited and Clark's Shoes Australia Limited.

The advent of large factories—powered by steam, gas and electricity, and owned by anonymous corporations—occurred at a relatively advanced stage in Collingwood's development, chiefly between 1880 and 1914. The corporate factories were a symptom of, as well as a contributing factor in, a continuing process. If the concept of 'industry' involves both business and technology, it was business rather than technology that laid the foundations for industrial Collingwood. These foundations were laid as early as 1838, but particularly in the 1850s and 1860s. They were laid by men of many occupations—land speculators, subdividers, builders, contractors, bootmakers, publicans, grocers, butchers, tanners, fellmongers, candlemakers, brewers, brickmakers and nightmen. These men did not have much to do with machinery; they were businessmen. And when technology became important in Collingwood (relatively late in the nineteenth century), it was directed to business ends. When people speak of 'industrial' inner suburbs, they really mean that these environments were created by commerce. When people speak of 'working-class' suburbs, they tend to forget that the most important decisions affecting these suburbs have always been made by businessmen—that is, by employers rather than employees.

Melbourne's population growth stopped during the depression of the 1890s. Many new villas in the outer suburbs remained empty, while householders in the inner suburbs were under pressure to sub-let rooms (in Collingwood, even stables and woodsheds)

M

and to take in boarders. The solid two-storey houses in southern Fitzroy were particularly suitable for subdividing into tenements.

After the depression, Collingwood Council resumed condemning old shacks left from the gold era. In the twelve years to 1912, there were 380 demolitions. More than 200 of these were to make way for the sprawling department store, warehouses and factories of the Foy and Gibson company on the Slope. The construction of the Melbourne–Collingwood direct railway in 1901 wiped out several streets on the Flat. Other demolitions were for large factories such as Whybrow Shoes. But this activity did not 'remove slums' completely. It probably contributed to a deterioration in other houses in Collingwood—and, significantly, in Fitzroy. As Herbert Gans, American sociologist and planner, has put it (in *People and Plans*, 1968), 'The slums cannot be emptied unless and until there is more low-cost housing elsewhere.' And, Gans says, 'the best way to eliminate slums is to eliminate poverty.'

Sometimes the condemned shacks in Collingwood were replaced by jerry-built wooden houses, but generally Collingwood's industries were developing at a faster rate than its residential facilities. With good tram and train services, Collingwood factories were able to draw on labour from other suburbs. In 1914 Collingwood's population was 36,240—an increase of only 1,170 over 1891.

The difference between Collingwood and the new eastern and southern middle-class suburbs such as Camberwell is summed up by Geoffrey Blainey in his *History of Camberwell* (1964). In the first decades of this century, Blainey says, Camberwell was eager to create an environment that differed from the inner suburbs:

> Camberwell fought industrialism, banned quarrying and refused to license noxious industries like the manufacturing of dripping. It upheld standards of housing, refusing to sanction shops or houses on small allotments, and refusing from 1898 to allow wooden houses to be built in an increasing number of streets. It fought blatant commercialism, prohibiting from 1916 the display of any advertisement that 'disfigures the beauty of any landscape in the District'. And it won its proudest victory when by popular vote it closed every hotel and wine saloon in the district.

While Camberwell became one of the most desirable suburbs in Australia, Collingwood was regarded as a source of evil. The most widely known citizen ever produced by Collingwood was probably John Wren (1871–1953). He had a typical Collingwood beginning, working first in a woodyard and then in the shoe industry. In 1893 he began an illegal totalizator business which, in depressed Colling-wood, developed into an important local industry. Like the river-side industrialists of the previous generation, he enjoyed local protection and managed to survive attempts by the State authori-ties to suppress his illegal activities. By the time his 'tote' was closed in 1906, Wren had begun acquiring considerable business interests throughout Australia. He also acquired a behind-the-scenes political influence. Throughout his career, opponents alleged that Wren was involved in shady business practices and in intimidation of policemen and politicians. To understand the rise of the Wren machine, it is helpful if we remember the suburb where he began—a poor suburb deprived of other, more legitimate means of power.

Much bad housing in the inner suburbs survived to the middle of the twentieth century, despite several public investigations. A Royal Commission on housing in 1914 heard evidence from inner-suburban citizens (including councillors, policemen and clergymen) who cited examples of the worst housing. (The Collingwood examples included some new houses being built by two councillors.) But nothing was done. In 1929 a Metropolitan Town Planning Commission, which had been established by the Victorian government, again drew attention to sub-standard housing —without result.

By the end of the boom of the 1920s, the inner suburbs had become dwarfed by rings of outer suburbs. Improved transport (electrification of tramways and railways and the increasing ownership of motor-cars) contributed to these changes. Clifton Hill and North Fitzroy fell in the social scale. Some outer suburbs, particularly to Melbourne's north and west, began to attract new factories. In general, the population of the inner suburbs decreased steadily from 1920, especially in Collingwood.

In the 1930s the inner suburbs again found themselves with concentrations of the unemployed, as in the 1890s. In 1936 the government appointed a Housing Investigation and Slum Abolition Board, which made a thorough survey of the inner suburbs. Despite political pressure, the Board in 1937 printed in alphabetical order twenty-five pages of the names of slum owners, many of whom were absentee landlords charging exorbitant rents. The names included churches, prominent citizens, even government or semi-government agencies. Following a public outcry over this, the government established the Victorian Housing Commission in 1938 to tackle the problem.

In the next three decades, the Housing Commission built tens of thousands of cottages in the outer suburbs for low-income families. This (together with improved economic conditions which also made new private housing available) resulted in an exodus from the inner suburbs after World War II. The vacancies in the inner suburbs were filled partly by the expansion of industry (including motor service stations and car storage space) but largely by European migrants, who renovated many of the old houses, thus arresting the process of blight.

Census figures show that Greek and Italian migrants alone accounted for 8 per cent of Collingwood's population in 1954 and 21 per cent in 1961. In addition there were migrants from Britain, Malta, Yugoslavia and dozens of other countries. In 1966 the population of Collingwood was down to 22,754—the lowest since the late 1870s. While Collingwood's population fell by 12 per cent between 1961 and 1966, the Australian-born component fell by 24 per cent and the overseas-born component rose by 13 per cent. Among the overseas-born a significant trend appeared in the 1960s: Collingwood lost many of its British-born migrants and some of its Italian-born, but had a big increase in the number of Yugoslav-born and an even bigger increase in the number of Greek-born.

Of students aged eleven or twelve entering Collingwood High School in 1969, 55 per cent came from homes where English was not generally spoken (with Greek predominating). Only two-thirds of the school's intake lived in a conventional family of two adults; one-third came from single-parent families or from families of up to six adults; 40 per cent of the families contained four or more children. Teachers affirm that, in Australia today, these circumstances may place a child at a considerable educational and vocational disadvantage, particularly where a school is inadequately staffed and equipped.[1]

During the 1960s the Housing Commission slowed down its construction of detached houses in the outer suburbs. Instead, working within policies laid down by the Victorian government, it began to concentrate on 'slum clearance' in the inner suburbs.[2] The methods used have resulted in much controversy.

The 1936–7 survey of inner-suburban housing, referred to earlier, involved a thorough house-to-house inspection, including interiors. Coloured maps showed bad houses interspersed with fair and good houses. But the Housing Commission in the 1950s and 1960s surveyed the exteriors rather than the interiors. It was concerned largely with the appearance of streets and the 'average condition' of the areas. In each inner suburb, it began demolishing not individual houses but a whole block. Under the block-clearance method, it is possible that the houses demolished will include some that have been renovated by migrants and some that could have been repaired if the government were to offer low-interest loans to owners. The proportion of these 'good' and 'fair' houses is probably small in Collingwood, but is substantial in Fitzroy and Carlton.

Understandably the Commission refuses to build detached houses on such expensive land. In Collingwood it has tried three different projects. We shall examine these in ascending order—low-rise, medium-rise and high-rise.

The low-rise project is an estate of thirty-six double-storey row-houses built in 1968 in Alexandra Parade, Clifton Hill. The rows are built around three sides of the cleared block. Each family has rooms both downstairs and upstairs (including three bedrooms and two toilets) and has its own small front and rear gardens. In the centre of the block, behind all the houses, half an acre of grassed common land has been kept as a children's playground. This row-housing is among the most widely-approved of the Commission's inner-suburban estates.

The other two projects in Collingwood are both situated in Portion 74. Originally subdivided and built on in 1853, this land was cited in the 1937 report as the worst concentration of substandard housing in Collingwood.

The medium-rise project, which accommodates about 1,000 people, comprises three-storey blocks of apartments. Built comparatively early (1958) with the limited funds available to the Commission, these apartments have a minimum of amenities. They have no garbage chutes or running hot water. The only laundries are communal and they necessitate the use of stairs—a frustrating task for a mother with young children. The Commission is considering ways to improve facilities in buildings of this vintage.

The high-rise project in Portion 74 comprises three twenty-storey blocks of apartments, built between 1967 and 1971. The first two blocks each contain 700 people; the third, 1,000 people. About half are children.

High-rise developments result in a big increase in residential density. Pre-demolition statistics for Portion 74 are unavailable, but the point can be illustrated from a high-rise development in 1968–72 in Gertrude Street, Fitzroy (Portion 49). The buildings demolished there contained 557 persons (a density of 33 persons per acre). The high-rise development there was planned to accommodate 3,024 persons (at 200 per acre). This is $5\frac{1}{2}$ times the previous population. The number of children in the area was expected to multiply by eight.

In comparison, the two-storey row-houses in Clifton Hill have a density of only about 70 persons per acre—that is, one-third as many persons per acre as the high-rise flats. Furthermore, the Commission says, the row-housing is more costly to provide (per family) than the high-rise.

By 1971, largely because of the Commission's activities, Collingwood's population decline appeared to be halting—at about 23,000. In earlier chapters it was noted that the businessmen who built the inner suburbs in the 1850s tended to regard streets as vast assembly lines for mass-producing customers and tenants. Something similar seems to be happening in the Housing Commission projects of today. In some ways, the Commission's skyscrapers are like vertical streets.

When the high-rise developments began in Collingwood, the first tenants tended to be mostly Australian-born. By 1970, because of comings and goings, the Australian-born component was about one-third and was decreasing. The overseas component was divided between British-born and European-born, with the latter increasing more rapidly. In the new Fitzroy high-rise development in 1970, Australian-born tenants accounted for 26 per cent, British-born 19 per cent and European 55 per cent.

A cartoonist's view of the Victorian government's slum-clearance methods.

Technically, the high-rise flats in Portion 74 have many advantages over the neighbouring medium-rise flats—for example, lifts, central heating, and running hot water. In addition to the communal laundries, each high-rise flat (unlike the medium-rise) has space for a washing machine. High-rise tenants are said to be more satisfied with their lot than the medium-rise tenants.

High-rise flats enable much of the cleared site to be kept as open space. Apart from car-parking, Collingwood's first two high-rise buildings share an open space of three acres. This includes children's playgrounds and also areas for practising basketball, cricket and football.

However, although the high-rise flats have solved some problems, they have also occasioned new ones. The population of Portion 74 was swollen overnight with numbers comparable to a country town, but the community facilities normally found in a town were not provided. The additional children had to crowd into the existing schools, which, according to teachers, were already sub-standard. Collingwood High School, for example, was a building that had been condemned before World War I. Apart from children's playgrounds (with fixed, tubular steel equipment), the housing estate in Portion 74 had no facilities for creative recreation for children, adolescents or adults. No supervisors were employed for the children's play areas. No social workers or youth workers were employed. The Housing Commission and Collingwood Council agreed that community facilities were needed, but disagreed over the financial arrangements, and so nothing was done. The situation in other inner suburbs was similar. The Housing Commission said that its job was to provide housing, and that other governmental, municipal and private agencies existed to deal with social welfare. Social workers, clergymen and teachers replied that better co-ordination was needed between the Housing Commission and the other agencies.[3]

There are further ramifications. By the late 1960s, in contrast to the previous era of absentee landlords, it was becoming common for inner-suburban cottages to be owned by their occupiers—especially European migrants. According to the most recent figures available from the Housing Commission, one area demolished in Richmond in the late 1960s consisted of 67 per cent owner-occupiers. But Commission flats are for renting, not for sale. Thus an area of owner-occupiers is converted to an area of tenants.

Earlier, we have seen how Collingwood first became a low-income area in the 1850s (chapter 2) and Fitzroy in the 1880s and

Traffic corridors through Melbourne's inner suburbs, 1985. The thick lines show the approximate location of proposed freeways. The broken lines show arterial roads with divided carriageways, based on existing roads.

N

1890s (chapter 9). Today, because Commission dwellings are available only to persons in the lowest income groups, these suburbs are being confirmed as low-income areas—systematically. Furthermore, because the tenantry is transient and is confined to the lowest income groups, it is likely to be handicapped in dealing with the large institutions that shape its destiny. In contrast to this, a significant development has occurred in recent years in Carlton. There, many houses have been rehabilitated by migrants, university people, city professional people and others. The new residents are developing a community spirit. They have formed a Carlton Association as a watch-dog, keeping an eye on the authorities. The Carlton Association is reminiscent of the suburban 'local committees' of the 1850s, described in chapter 3. There are signs, too, of a possible civic re-awakening in several other inner suburbs. In Fitzroy and Collingwood, the vanguard consists of young clergymen who have become involved in the social problems of their district.

The Housing Commission is not the only institution that is determining the future shape of the inner suburbs. During the 1960s the Victorian government commissioned a survey of Melbourne transport needs to 1985. According to the published report, the *Melbourne Transportation Study* (1969), the Housing Commission's estates would be surrounded increasingly by busy roads. In Collingwood three new freeways were to be constructed. Two would be in a north-south direction: the F-1 (six lanes) parallel with Wellington Street and Smith Street and the F-2 (eight lanes) parallel with Hoddle Street. The high-rise estate in Portion 74 is situated between these two proposed freeways. The third freeway, running east-west, would be the Eastern Freeway (the F-19) of up to eight lanes. It would run along Alexandra Parade—that is, past the front doors of the Housing Commission's two-storey row-houses. The F-1 and F-19 were each expected to carry 60,000 to 100,000 vehicles through Collingwood daily. The F-2 was expected to carry more than 130,000 vehicles daily. The report did not indicate whether the freeways would be at (or above or below) ground level, but in any case the structures would divide Collingwood into islands.

The freeways would mean more than merely six or eight lanes. There would be entrances, exits and junctions, requiring ramps and viaducts. And the effect of the traffic would not stop at the kerbside. Noise and air pollution would create a 'dead' area for several hundred yards beside the roads.

In addition, it was being planned that some existing roads would be widened in order to carry more traffic through Collingwood. Two of these (Hoddle Street and Wellington Street) are the eastern and western boundaries of Portion 74. Indeed, the widening of Hoddle Street was to take a slice (70 ft wide) from the open space on the Housing Commission estate. Another road being considered for widening was Johnston Street, which is only a couple of hundred yards from the estate. The estate was in danger of becoming a kind of ghetto for pedestrians.

The freeways and road-widenings were expected to subtract from Collingwood's meagre parklands. The F-19 would wipe out a grassed reserve that exists along the middle of Alexandra Parade. The widening of Hoddle Street would take a slice from the Darling Gardens in Clifton Hill. Tentative plans for the F-2 showed it going through the Mayor's Park in Clifton Hill.

The *Transportation Study* predicted that the percentage of car-owning households would be smaller in the inner suburbs than in the middle-class outer suburbs. In other words, Collingwood would continue to serve as a receptacle for refuse—in this case, a receptacle for other people's noise and smog.

The *Transportation Study* also predicted that not only would the population decline in Collingwood, Fitzroy and Richmond be arrested but also that by 1985 there would be an increase of 29 per cent over the 1964 population. In view of the intrusions by industry and traffic, it is difficult to see where the authorities expect to house these additional people—unless it is in more high-rise flats. Judging from experience so far, one can foresee difficulties in providing these people with the community facilities (education, creative recreation and social welfare) that are becoming normal expectations in the space age. Regardless of the merits and demerits of high-density public-housing projects, it has yet to be demonstrated that the best place to build them is on an island between motor speedways.

NOTES

The original manuscript was heavily footnoted. The following notes are a small selection. As there is no point in directing the general reader to material which is not available to the public, these notes are confined chiefly to printed material, and they refer chiefly to major issues or substantial quotations. Researchers wishing to follow up details or particular issues are welcome to contact the author.

1 Suburbia in Australia

1 Asa Briggs, 'The sociology of Australian cities', *Outlook*, Sydney, August 1961.
2 'Urban Australia', in A. F. Davies and S. Encel, *Australian Society: A sociological introduction* (Melbourne, 2nd ed., 1970). See also *Australian Economic History Review*, vol. 10, no. 2 (1970) (special issue, 'Urbanization in Australia').
3 Robert Park, Ernest W. Burgess and Roderick D. McKenzie, *The City* (Chicago, 1925).
4 A. A. Congalton, *Status and Prestige in Australia* (Melbourne, 1969).
5 'A social ranking of Melbourne suburbs', *Australian and New Zealand Journal of Sociology*, vol. 3 (1967); F. L. Jones, *Dimensions of Urban Social Structure: the social areas of Melbourne* (Canberra, 1969). See also G. R. Bruns, 'Some neglected aspects of Melbourne's demography', unpubl. M.A. thesis, University of Melbourne, 1949.
6 E.g., James Grant and Geoffrey Serle, *The Melbourne Scene 1803-1956* (Melbourne, 1957), p. 204.
7 'Suburbia: community and network', in Davies and Encel, op. cit., p. 302.
8 'The slums of Victorian London', in *Victorian Studies*, vol. 10, no. 1 (September 1967).

2 The birth of two suburbs

1 *Argus*, 3 December 1850; see also 17 October 1848; 1 June 1849; 1 February, 5 December 1850; 5 November 1851.
2 Ibid., 20, 3 May 1852; see also letter, 7 May 1852.
3 Ibid., 13 May 1855.
4 11 March 1865; see also 11 August 1866.
5 A similar, but not identical, re-arrangement of occupations is used by Graeme Davison in an unpublished B.A. thesis on Richmond, Victoria, submitted to the Department of History, University of Melbourne, 1962.
6 *Streetcar Suburbs* (Boston, 1962), pp. 172-3. For Boston, 1870-1905, Warner estimates that no census figures can be taken as more accurate than plus or minus 6 per cent.
7 Royal Commission on housing, 1914, evidence by Collingwood town clerk.
8 Housing Investigation and Slum Abolition Board, first report, 1937.
9 16 May, 12, 14 July 1855; see also reminiscences in *Melbourne Church News*, 17 July 1866, and *Observer*, 20 March 1874.
10 9 June, 16 July 1853.
11 Chief Secretary's Records, Vic. State Archives, letter R55/15665.
12 13, 20 August 1864.

3 The suburban frontier

1 *Argus*, 23 January 1854.
2 Ibid., 15 July 1854.
3 Ibid., 12, also 6-16 July 1855.
4 Ibid., 8 June 1857.
5 In the remainder of this chapter, the chief sources are the minute books of Collingwood Council. These have been checked against other sources, including the Chief Secretary's Records in the State Archives and reports in newspapers. Of the many press reports, the north-south rivalry is best seen in the *Argus*, 19 February 1856.
6 9 July 1885.
7 30 August, 8 March 1862.
8 *Observer*, 22 November 1862; Collingwood ratebook, 1864, pp. 55-6.
9 For comparative data from the U.S.A., see: N. M. Blake, *Water for the Cities* (Syracuse, N.Y., 1956), p. 269; Blake McKelvey, *The Urbanization of America* (New Brunswick, N.J., 1963), p. 13; R. S. and H. M. Lynd, *Middletown* (New York, 1929), p. 97.

4 The suburb with bad breath

1 Central Board of Health reports; also Select Committee on night-soil, 1866.
2 *Observer*, 24 January 1863.
3 *Melbourne Church News*, 17 July 1866. For an interesting discussion of the social role of the 'bad smell', see F. M. Jones, 'The aesthetic of the nineteenth-century town', in H. J. Dyos (ed.), *The Study of Urban History* (London, 1968).
4 *Argus*, 29 December 1860 to 3 January 1861.
5 31 January 1863. For comparative information about economizers in English municipalities, see Asa Briggs, *Victorian Cities* (Harmondsworth, 1968), pp. 210-11, 373; and W. H. Chaloner, *The Social and Economic Development of Crewe 1780-1923* (Manchester, 1950), pp. 121, 125.
6 18 February 1865.

5 From cesspits to cesspans

1 *Argus*, 17 July 1854.
2 *Observer*, 16 January 1864.

3 Select Committee on the Yan Yean Tramroad, pp. 15-16.
4 10 and (editorial) 16 February 1866.
5 *Observer*, 8 September 1870.
6 Central Board of Health, 16th report, in *Victorian Parliamentary Papers*, 1876, vol. 3, p. 9. See also editorials in *Observer*, 25 March 1875, and *Age*, 3 April 1875. The twenty-two C.B.H. reports, 1855-89, are the major source for this chapter, supplemented by other parliamentary papers and the Collingwood Council minute books.

6 Industry and the River Yarra

1 Royal Commission on noxious trades, 1870-1.
2 Geoffrey Serle, *The Golden Age* (Melbourne, 1963), pp. 247, 289.
3 7 January 1909.
4 *Age*, 10 September 1864. See also *Observer*, 13 May 1897—a Collingwood version of Protectionist history. My reconstruction of C. J. Don's movements is based on searches in the Collingwood Council minutes, the ratebook, the Sands and McDougall *Melbourne Directory*, *Hansard* and newspapers.
5 *Observer*, 17 October 1896 (useful biography of Richard Cooke, builder and political activist).
6 17 March 1866. An article on J. W. Randall in the *Observer*, 5 May 1904, gives information about bribery of parliamentarians in the 1860s.
7 February-March 1865.
8 *Observer*, 6 August 1874. This later period is treated in T. G. Parsons, 'Some aspects of manufacturing in Melbourne, 1870-90', Ph.D. thesis, Department of History, Monash University, 1970.

7 The death of the River Yarra

1 When research began for this book, there was no known list of Collingwood councillors for the nineteenth century. To compile one, I sifted through the council minute books, noting by-elections as well as general elections. For the council's first quarter-century (1855-81), the total

number of councillors came to sixty-seven. I kept a card for each man and, throughout my research, gradually added details of his occupation, property and municipal career. In Table 7, the calculations refer to the situation at the beginning of each municipal year.

2 *Victorian Hansard*, 1861-2, vol. 8; 1864-5, vol. 11; *Victorian Parliamentary Debates*, 1866, vol. 2; 1867, vol. 3.

3 *Age, Argus*, 11 March 1865.

4 3 June 1865.

5 *Argus*, 12 March 1869.

6 14 September 1868.

8 From cesspans to sewerage

1 *Herald*, 6-12 April 1869.

2 *Observer*, 25 March 1875, June and October 1876.

3 *Argus*, 16-18 October 1875; *Observer*, 21 October 1875; C.B.H. report, 1876.

4 20 September 1883; also 9 July, 10 September 1874.

5 For revisions made in the miasma theory by 1888, see the first report of the Royal Commission on Melbourne sanitation, 1889, p. xxxiii.

6 Blake McKelvey, *The Urbanization of America* (New Brunswick, N.J., 1963), p. 90; Constance Green, *The Rise of Urban America* (London, 1966), p. 106.

7 Gordon Greenwood and John Laverty, *Brisbane 1858-1959* (Brisbane, 1959).

9 Suburbs in transition

1 *Observer*, 7 May 1891; *Herald*, 30 April 1891. For the context of Melbourne in the 1880s, see Geoffrey Serle, *A History of the Colony of Victoria, 1883-1889* (Melbourne, 1971).

2 28 September 1867.

3 P. J. Rimmer, 'The boot and shoe industry in Melbourne', in *The Australian Geographer*, vol. 10 (1968).

10 The inner suburbs today

1 Typewritten report, 1969, by F. P. Golding, teacher, Collingwood High School.

2 Annual reports of the Housing Commission, Victoria. See also Anne Stevenson, Elaine Martin and Judith O'Neill, *High Living: a Study of Family Life in Flats* (Melbourne, 1967). I am grateful to Mr R. Burkitt, member of the Housing Commission, for some information used in this chapter.

3 Victorian Council of Social Service, *Report on Community and Welfare Facilities in Fitzroy* (Melbourne, 1969). See also Ronald F. Henderson, Alison Harcourt and R. J. A. Harper, *People in Poverty: A Melbourne Survey* (Melbourne, 1970). High-rise developments in Britain have been satirized by Patrick Goldring in *The Broilerhouse Society* (London, 1969). For criticisms of Australian public housing, see Hugh Stretton, *Ideas for Australian Cities* (Adelaide, 1970), and M. A. Jones, 'The Role of the Australian State Housing Authorities in Low Income Housing', unpubl. Ph.D. thesis, Australian National University, Canberra, 1971.

SOURCES

The chief source materials used in this research project are located at the following institutions: the La Trobe Library in the State Library of Victoria; the State Archives in the State Library of Victoria; the Victorian Parliamentary Library; the Registrar General's Office, Victoria; the Lands Department, Victoria; Collingwood Town Hall; Fitzroy Town Hall; Melbourne Town Hall; the Baillieu Library, University of Melbourne.

VICTORIAN GOVERNMENT RECORDS (MANUSCRIPT)

Titles Office records on land ownership, Registrar General's Office, Melbourne.

Records of the Chief Secretary's Office (inwards correspondence, including letters from municipal councils), 1851 onwards, State Archives.

Defunct Companies Records, State Archives.

VICTORIAN OFFICIAL PAPERS (PRINTED)

Census of Victoria, 1851 onwards.

Reports of the Central Board of Health, 1855-89.

Reports of the Board of Public Health, 1891 onwards.

Reports from select committees of parliament, royal commissions and boards of inquiry. The major reports studied were the following: on the sewerage of Melbourne, 1852-3; on public baths, 1856-7; on the tariff, 1859-60; on the East Collingwood Improvement Bill, 1862-3; on manufactures, 1864-5; on the Yan Yean Tramroad, 1866; on nightsoil, 1866; on noxious trades, 1870; on the sewerage of Melbourne, 1871; on diphtheria, 1872; on the tariff, 1883; on shops, 1884; on the sanitary condition of Melbourne, 1889, 1890; on housing conditions, 1914 (published 1917, 1918); on housing investigation and slum abolition, 1937. These reports were traced through J. M. Worthington's index to Victorian parliamentary papers.

Victorian Hansard, 1861-4, and *Victorian Parliamentary Debates,* 1865 onwards.

Victorian Government Gazette.

MUNICIPAL RECORDS (MANUSCRIPT)

Collingwood Council minute books, 1855 onwards.

Collingwood Council rate assessment books, 1864 onwards.
Collingwood Council sanitary inspector's report books, 1885 onwards.
Health Committee minute books, Melbourne City Council, 1869 onwards.

MAPS AND PLANS

Plans of Melbourne and suburbs, 1838 onwards, Victorian Lands Department.
Maps and plans in Historical Collection, La Trobe Library.
Vale and Company collection of real estate plans, La Trobe Library.
Melbourne and Metropolitan Board of Works sewerage plans, 1897, Lands Department.
Plans of subdivisions, drainage and paving, in Collingwood City Engineer's Office.

DIRECTORIES

Victorian Parliamentary electoral rolls, 1856.
Melbourne directories (Sands and Kenny, 1857-61; Sands and McDougall, 1862 onwards).
Victorian Municipal Directory, 1875 onwards.

NEWSPAPERS

Observer (Collingwood and Fitzroy), 1862-1909 (temporarily renamed the *Manufacturer* in 1867).
Mercury (Collingwood, Fitzroy and northern suburbs).
Argus (Melbourne), 1846 onwards.
Age (Melbourne), 1861 onwards.
Herald (Melbourne), 1861 onwards.
Daily Telegraph (Melbourne), 1869 onwards.
For this research, all available issues of the *Observer* (from 1862 to 1909) were searched from cover to cover. Reports in the Melbourne press were traced by means of clues obtained from other sources—e.g., from the Collingwood Council minutes, from the *Observer* and (for 1846-58) from J. A. Feely's *Argus Index*. In addition, certain articles in daily newspapers and in periodicals were traced through card indexes in the research department of the La Trobe Library.

INDEX

Abattoirs, 73, 92-4
Adelaide, 6, 8, 136
Aitken, Thomas, 95, 100, 101-3, 108, 160
Alexander, Charles, 92-4, 126

Baker, Charles, 67
Bank of Australasia, 20
Baths, 44, 53
Bent, Thomas, 156
Berry, Graham, 60, 103, 104, 109
Berry, Joseph, 61
Botany Bay, 5-6, 11
Breweries, 11, 51, 94-7, 159-61
Brickmakers, 11, 97, 113-14, 118
Bridges, *see* Roads and bridges
Brighton, 41, 146, 152
Brisbane, 6, 10, 74, 136
Brunswick, 84
Brunswick Street (Fitzroy), 17, 20, 21, 37, 67, 152, 154
Building industry, 24, 31-3, 40, 43
Butchers, 50, 91-4; *see also* Abattoirs; Industry; Livestock

Camberwell, 40, 152, 162
Carlton, 3, 6, 8, 21, 40, 41, 46, 113, 145-7, 166, 170
Central Board of Health, 28, 35, 55-7, 72-86, 91, 92, 114-20, 125-39
Central drain, 15, 35, 44, 45, 51, 57; *see also* Drainage
Central Road Board, 35, 39, 41
Cesspits, *see* Sanitation
Children, 10, 34-5, 141-3; mortality, 56
Church Street, 41
Churches, 30, 34, 38; Anglican, 67-8
Clark, Benjamin, 100
Clifton Hill, 15, 39, 44-5, 50, 53, 65, 66, 86, 140-7, 152, 164, 171
Collingwood, 3; case study, 8-13, 37; created a city, 148; gold mine, 104; local government, 10, 39; local committees, 38-40, 46, 169; name, 14, 123; population, 10, 24, 50, 140, 161-5, 171; settlement, 19-25
Collingwood Council, alleged malpractices, 43, 48; elections, 42, 100, 147; factions, 42-9, 59-61, 100, 101-2, 148, 151, 154; public works committee, 45, 49-50
Collingwood Gas Company, 53, 109
Cooke, Richard, 49
Crooke, William, 97, 100, 118, 129
Crown land, 14, 39, 44, 53, 65, 66

Dehnert, Robert, 105, 108, 148
Dight family, 15, 155-9
Don, Charles Jardine, 60, 100, 101-3, 109
Drainage, 15, 35, 37, 44-6, 57-60, 64, 104-5; *see also* Central drain; Reilly Street; Sanitation

Eade, Joel, 157
East Collingwood, *see* Collingwood
East Collingwood Improvement Bill, 59, 102
Eastern Hill, 14, 18
Elizabeth Street, (Collingwood), 59, 61, 64, 101-2
Embling, Thomas, 99, 109, 111
Emerald Hill, *see* South Melbourne

Fawkner, John Pascoe, 41, 42, 43, 88
Fellmongers, *see* Noxious trades
FitzGibbon, E. G., 131, 151
Fitzroy, 3, 12; case study, 8-9; created a city, 148; development in 1860s, 61-4, 66, 74-5, 76; in 1880-1900, 123-4, 126, 139, 145-7, 150-7, 162; local government, 10, 14, 21, 39, 45; population, 20, 24; settlement, 6, 14-21
Flemington, 39, 78, 145
Flockhart, Robert, 100
Foresters, *see* Lodges
Foy, Mark, 52, 103, 162
Free Trade, *see* Protection and Free Trade
Freemasons, *see* Lodges

Garbage disposal, *see* Sanitation
Gas supply, 52; *see also* Collingwood Gas Company; Melbourne Gas Company